BREAD FOR THE SOUL

BREAD for the Soul

Stories That Nourish, Comfort, and Heal

Jim Clarke

Paulist Press
New York / Mahwah, NJ

Cover design by Joe Gallagher
Book design by Lynn Else

Library of Congress Cataloging-in-Publication Data
Names: Clarke, Jim (Clergyman), author.
Title: Bread for the soul : stories that nourish, comfort, and heal / Jim Clarke.
Description: New York; Mahwah, NJ: Paulist Press, [2024] | Includes bibliographical references. | Summary: "Using stories as an entry, and in an easy, conversational style, Jim Clarke covers a wide range of questions, dilemmas, and concerns that arise in the ordinary, everyday lives of the people of God"—Provided by publisher.
Identifiers: LCCN 2023030627 (print) | LCCN 2023030628 (ebook) | ISBN 9780809156771 (paperback) | ISBN 9780809188406 (ebook)
Subjects: LCSH: Bible stories, English. | Christian life.
Classification: LCC BV4501.3 .C5247 2024 (print) | LCC BV4501.3 (ebook) | DDC 248.4—dc23/eng/20231220
LC record available at https://lccn.loc.gov/2023030627
LC ebook record available at https://lccn.loc.gov/2023030628

ISBN 978-0-8091-5677-1 (paperback)
ISBN 978-0-8091-8840-6 (e-book)

Published by Paulist Press
997 Macarthur Boulevard
Mahwah, New Jersey 07430
www.paulistpress.com

Printed and bound in the United States of America

Dedicated to all the great storytellers of
ancient and modern times, across cultures, languages,
and continents, who have graced us down the
years with the precious gift of Story

Contents

CONTENTS

Preface

At the beginning of every episode of *Star Trek: The Next Generation*, Patrick Stewart intones:

> To explore strange new worlds.
> To seek out new life and new civilizations.
> To boldly go where no one has gone before.

These are the places to which stories take us. Capturing and challenging our imagination, stories help us to reach out beyond ourselves and at the same time deep within ourselves—to seek, to explore, and to go to new places. The way we imagine our lives through stories is the way we go on living our lives. Stories form us.

As the Talmud says so eloquently, God loves stories so much that God created human beings. Stories enliven us, encourage us, and give meaning to the details of our lives. Stories have been a fundamental way, over the ages, in which we human beings have communicated our values and desires. In this book, I will use the medium of stories to explore the wisdom of our societal cultural experiences and to unpack our own individual learned lessons. As a story is told, it can bring comfort to the confused or heartbroken, nourish the unspoken dream or wish of an adolescent, inspire a tired heart, or heal a wounded soul. How a story is expressed can imprison, unshackle, and/or heal both the storyteller and the audience. Traditional storytellers have always been held in high esteem for their ability to connect audiences with the deeper truths of life, as well as their own individual reality.

God enters the human story from within and gives us a different perspective or experience of what it means to be human. Jesus's stories and parables were revolutionary because they invited listeners to enter their own stories with a different viewpoint—to see as God sees. Like St. Paul, we are to enter the Christ story and see and experience our lives from a brand-new place.

Ideally, stories are meant to liberate, expand, and authenticate the human person and condition. This is narrative theology and active imagination at its best. Classical mythology (that is, cultural stories from the ages) offers us a sacred psychology of collected wisdom that acts as a template for our own storied struggles and reveals imaginative ways of healing resolution.

Stories that we are attracted to, identify with, or give allegiance to speak to the depths of who we are. They name us. We return to them often, to be assured and encouraged. These stories can be adventure stories, romantic films, religious scriptures, political stories of conspiracies and lies, or deep truths. Do the stories objectify, humanize, liberate, animate, or heal us? What stories do we tell about ourselves, others, or various groups of people?

Stories are imaginal ways of entering the human situation. American journalist and film critic David Denby says, "A story is not a version of life but an interpretation of experience; it's a way of telling, not a way of being, and it reverberates in every direction." Stories play many roles in our lives. They inform, form, and transform us, offering us a variety of entry points. Stories can come to us packaged as movies, novels, history, poetry, jokes, therapy, medical histories, or even as gossip. Our souls feed on stories.

Stories are patterned ways of expressing internal truths. Certain stories engage us at a deep level because in some way they reflect a part of our own story. That is why we sometimes find that we cannot put down a certain novel, forget a particular movie, or leave an engaging conversation.

All stories are true to one degree or another; some of them actually happened. We change our stories to fit the context of the situation or the audience. There is, however, a danger of focusing on the simple narrative without responding or respecting the multiplicity and complexity of the overlapping stories within. Think of the present political climate. We are invited to walk around in the story, try on different characters' roles and discover how they fit us.

The work of transformation can take place in the reframing or reenacting of the story. Many people who have experienced deep trauma in their lives struggle with moving from a victim stance in life to a more empowering perspective of their story. As Anglican Archbishop Desmond Tutu said, "It is not the trauma that defines us but the meaning that we make of the experience that defines who we are and who we ultimately become."

We always have a choice as to how we respond to pain or trauma. Victimization is an event; being a victim is a choice. Telling the story is how we get our dignity back after trauma. To keep the secret pain of the story inside us without adequate expression imprisons us and often makes us sick, according to Swiss psychoanalyst, Alice Miller. Rumi says it well in his poem, "Story Water":

> A story is like water
> That you heat for your bath.
>
> It takes messages between the fire
> And your skin. It lets them meet,
> And it cleans you!
>
> Very few can sit down
> In the middle of the fire itself

Like a salamander or Abraham.
We need intermediaries.

The way a story is told usually says a lot more about the storyteller than the tale. A story can be told repetitively as a means to protect the literal truth or the underlying feeling (such as lies); or it can be told creatively as a way of engaging the meaning significance of the story (such as theatre); or it can be shared as a therapeutic means of healing and reconciliation (for example, counseling).

Sometimes a story needs to be translated or deciphered for the audience to understand it or get the message. Many years ago when I was a young priest in a very busy parish, twenty-five-year-old Maria approached me and told me that she was dying of leukemia. She was a single woman who wanted to walk down the church aisle in a white dress before she died. I did not understand the real need underneath the request. So, sadly for both of us, I refused her request with these offhand words: "Maria, if we did this for you, we would have to do it for every single woman who wanted this favor." Her story has stayed with me and was the impetus for my own transformation as I studied the field of mythology—the stories of becoming human. Now I understand that Maria was asking me to help her develop a ritual of honoring her life before her death. I failed her.

Because we fail to mythologize, we tend to pathologize. What do I mean by that? We have a human need to tap into the great stories and myths of the universe by reading, learning, and reflecting on the world's scriptures, cultural myths, and human history in general. This mythologizing or meaning making will lead us to see connections for our pain and suffering. It brings order out of chaos. In this way, we move beyond the literal personal story to the larger cosmic story and hopefully to the deeper experience of our humanity. Another way to view this is, we are invited to observe our life not as physical or medical history but as soul history. In the first mode, life is seen as a problem to be solved or fixed medicinally; in the second, the path is experienced as an awakening, where everything is nourishment for the journey.

Explorations in science and technology must be balanced by explorations in imagination and creativity, to help the human community move forward. In the Salinas Valley State Prison in California, a Level 4 maximum prison, many of the prisoners are learning the tools to tell their stories and find meaning for their transformation. Their hearts are opened in this process of being "humanized."

This book is a reflection on many of the questions that I have received over the years from parishioners, directees, and students. Their yearning for understanding and wisdom on how to live their lives with faith, hope, and a measure of love has been encouraging to me.

Now I offer this book as a means for you to more fully enter the story of your own life with a wakefulness that will allow you to re-create your perspective, and therefore, your experience of yourself. Bring your questions and sense of wonder as we begin this journey. You are not alone. God, the great storyteller and dream maker, will accompany you on this adventure.

Shall we begin?

CHAPTER 1

What Are You Looking For?

There is a story told about Nasruddin who had lost his keys and was looking for them outside in the dark. He was patiently scanning the ground on his hands and knees, under the streetlamp in front of his house. A neighbor of his noticed his predicament and began to help him in his search. After a while, the neighbor asked Nasruddin, "Are you sure you lost your keys here?" "No," he said, "I lost them over there," pointing to a place some distance away. "Then why are we looking for the keys here?" persisted the man. "Because the light is much better here," replied Nasruddin.

Here is the first important question: "What are YOU looking for?" In John 1, Jesus asks this very question of his early disciples. Their answer leads Jesus to invite them to follow him. All of us are looking for something. Human beings have multiple needs for contentment and fulfillment. The list can include:

- Success (accomplishments)
- Security (physical and emotional)
- Peace and harmony
- Stability of relationships (felt sense of being connected)
- Protection (safety)
- Salary (earned recognition)
- Recognition (status or connections)
- Acceptance (feeling of belonging)

- Possessions (ownership)
- Encounter with God (connection with the Creator)
- Experience of awe and wonder (feeling of one's place in the cosmos)
- Intimacy (connection with significant others)
- Looking for the new and different (challenges)

Ultimately, every human being is looking for love, acceptance, and respect in some form. Each of us will go about this search throughout our lives in different ways. The next crucial question is: *Are we looking in the right place?*

Some of us look in appropriate places and others are drawn to unhealthy paths. We all are confronted with a menu of possibilities to find what works best for us. Some of these choices are not honest or healthy.

Some examples are:

- Performance orientation (Love me for what I do)
- Being super nice (Love me for how I present myself)
- Codependency (I will do anything and everything for you)
- Rumor mongering (I have all the information you need to know about everybody else)
- Obsession with appearance (Love me for how I look)

Most of us do not live in a specific community, but when people do live in a defined community, it is often possible to see this process at work. Take a retirement community where people have come to live together in a defined social setting. Some will seek acceptance by sharing their skills, others by social connections. Others might seek love and respect for their knowledge and intelligence, while yet others will share their hospitality and care.

What do you observe in the people around you? All behavior is needs-directed and one of our basic needs is to be loved and respected, which is healthy and universal. Some people seek out this response by being right, humorous, helpful, obedient, or good listeners. To be liked or loved we tend to do one or more of these actions. There is nothing wrong with this as long as it is genuine.

Recently, I watched a nature documentary that portrayed various wild animals in their daily interactions in their natural habitats. I was particularly struck by a mating ritual performed by two beautiful large seabirds. They faced each other with their huge twelve-foot wing spans completely extended, literally displaying their "undersides," and offered themselves as they were, so to speak. This ritual dance went on for five days. Now I am not suggesting this extreme for human beings, but what struck me was the willingness to be vulnerable to the other without artifice. They simply were who they were.

The final question is: *Are your own emotional needs being met in a satisfying way?* Often we can feel resentful when our needs are not being met, expecting others to fulfill us. No one person can do this for us, not our partner, not our spouse, not even our own family members. Ultimately, it is not all about me; it is about me acting in a healthy and honest way with the people in my life. At the same time, it is also about living a more genuine, fulfilling life from the inside out.

You'll know when you've found it.

Reflection Questions

1. Am I looking in the right place for fulfillment?
2. Do I really know what my deepest desire is?
3. Do I need a particular person to help me in this quest?

CHAPTER 2

How Can I Make My Life Sacred?

One day a rabbi was invited to a festive occasion to celebrate the birthday of a young member of his congregation. As the time drew near for the meal to begin, the rabbi was asked to bless the food. He walked to the banquet table, overflowing with a variety of dishes, turned to the gathered guests, and said gently, "You ask me to bless this food that the Creator has already made holy by its very existence? No, I think not." And he returned to his seat.

We often miss the most obvious of sacred blessings—food, rain, warmth, sleep, and friendship—because we can take them for granted. Sacredness is about awareness—awareness of the Divine in the present moment or experience. We also think of sacredness when we dedicate something ordinary for a higher purpose. For example, words become sacred when they are delivered with respect, gentleness, and authenticity. These words can be called prayers, vows, or promises, depending upon the person with whom they are shared, and the occasion or situation.

To create a sacred space or time is to intentionally dedicate it for a specific purpose. An example might be a special meal, a celebratory event, or a common gathering. The key is intentionality. Many of us live our lives moving from one task to another without much forethought. I invite you to live more consciously from the inside out, rather than from the outside in. Our value system resides in our interior life. This shift in perspective will help you to see everything and everyone differently. This is what Jesus preached as he saw reality as a manifestation of the Divine. He would use ordinary examples from people's lives as metaphors for the interior life. He often chided the crowds for looking, but not seeing clearly the hand of God and for listening, but not understanding (Matt 13:14).

What does the sacred feel like or look like? We find it in the experience of beauty, goodness, truth, or love that permeates a situation or an encounter. It often evokes a sense of awe or wonder in the observer. Some examples are walking in a forest, looking into the face of your newborn child, discovering a communion of hearts, having a significant conversation, and experiencing contemplative union.

If you want a more formal sacralization process, the church offers a series of rites called sacraments that celebrate this process:

- Cleansing (Baptism)
- Affirmation (Confirmation)
- Nourishment (Eucharist)
- Forgiveness (Penance)
- Illness (Sacrament of the Sick)
- Union (Marriage)
- Service (Holy Orders)

On this topic, psychotherapist Thomas Moore has written a very helpful book entitled *The Re-Enchantment of Everyday Life*, in which he invites the reader to examine his/her life through the lens of the sacred. Some of his areas of focus include the home, politics, art, stories, sex, and dreams.

What are some other ways in which we can sacralize our lives? Many people find these practices helpful:

- Observing a weekly "Sabbath" day of genuine rest
- Disconnecting from social media for a set period of time
- Reaching out to those in need through word or action
- Maintaining the discipline of leisure and play
- Sustaining a daily practice of solitude and silence
- Creating spaces of color and beauty in the home or office
- Blessing others with kind words of affirmation

I know well that this list of suggestions may seem overwhelming, but I encourage you to start small and build on your successes. My parents taught me how to do this from the time I was very young. They made time in their busy lives for the work of making holy the day because it was based on their firm belief that God is immersed in all that is.

How about you? How can you creatively sacralize your life? This is an important priority if you desire to bring greater depth and meaning to your life.

Let me give you an example of a memorable sacralizing event that took place in our family.

Upon the death of my parents, we siblings decided to sell the family house of fifty-six years. This was no small task as all eleven of us each had had their own memories of the house and how it should be dealt with. I persuaded my siblings and their families to participate in a "house cooling" ritual as a preamble to its sale. We all gathered one fine Saturday in the fall to share and cherish our experiences there. As we proceeded from room to room, we sat and spoke of our time together in those spaces, made sacred by our very presence as a large family. We laughed and cried as we recounted numerous memories. When we came to the back porch laundry of the house, one of my eight brothers recounted the story of our mother complaining about the amount of dirt on our sports uniforms. After listening to her, he said, “Well, Mom, that’s how you know that we are good athletes. We give our best on the field.” Said she, “I just wish that you would leave the dirt where it belongs—on the field and not on your clothes!”

Each sibling had a chance to bless a room with holy water and one of their children carried a blessed candle. We even blessed the garage, which had been converted into a dormitory and play space, and the yard—our rough and tumble arena—with our stories. Afterward, we sensed that by sharing our memories of the home we shared for so many years, we had fixed the home in our hearts. But now it was just a house, a building ready to be sold. Interestingly, none of us have felt the need to return. It was a sacred farewell that bonded us even more deeply as siblings.

Reflection Questions

1. Do I have a special place that I call “sacred”?
2. How do I make “holy the day”?
3. Do I plan my dinner conversations?

CHAPTER 3

How Do I Live with Balance in My Life?

There is a funny story told about a tightrope walker who came to town to advertise his daring cross-canyon walk the following week. As you can imagine there was a lot of hype about it, and the whole town turned out to see if Miguel could perform this incredible feat without falling. With much fanfare, Miguel made it across the deep canyon, walking ever so slowly across the thin wire. Not to be outdone, he asked the crowd if they thought he could do it while pushing a wheelbarrow. They all responded with a loud chorus of affirmation. So, he gladly repeated his exploit. The third time he asked the crowd if they believed he could do it with some weight in the wheelbarrow. They were beside themselves with excitement and awe at the possibility of Miguel accomplishing this. One man in particular was overly exuberant in his encouragement to Miguel. "I know you can do this," he said. Miguel calmly responded, "Then get in the wheelbarrow, my friend." The man declined.

Many people are looking for balance in their life, but few are willing to do the work. To achieve balance, you must practice a particular type of discipline that will accomplish this goal.

What are the values that you would like to enhance in your life? What do you want to avoid?

Virtue is always balanced by two vices, one on either side. For example, humility is balanced by hubris (thinking too much of yourself) on the one side and devaluing (thinking too little of oneself) on the other side. We are to avoid both extremes. Every sacred "yes" needs a sacred "no" to guard the desired result.

After your reflection, I encourage you to write down in your journal what is most important to you. How often do you engage in this behavior? What do you need to let go of to do it more often? What change do you need to make to accomplish this resolution?

I remember a terribly busy time in my ministerial career when I knew I needed and wanted more time for prayer and for exercise. I felt constrained by the expectations of others and by my own ambitions. However, after a concentrated time of reflection, I realized the only way I could achieve this goal was if I changed my daily schedule. So, I decided to watch less TV and go to bed earlier. This then gave me the time to rise earlier for prayer and spiritual reading, followed by regular exercise. I am happy to say I have faithfully followed this discipline for many years now. It has been immensely helpful in keeping me emotionally balanced and spiritually grounded.

What about you? What can you change in your daily schedule that can set you on the right course? Small changes can contribute to greater course corrections in the long term. Moderation in all things sustains us in the long run.

The question of proper balance is especially important in regard to guiding the pace of our busy lives. I find that it helps me to build into my schedule regular "buffer" times to allow for the unplanned, unexpected events of life. By doing this, I don't race from one engagement to another. This practice reminds me that I am not God; I cannot do everything. I can only be present to this moment, this encounter. When I do that, I am much more peaceful and grounded. Are you happy with the pace of your life? If not, what changes can you make?

One traditional weekly practice that can serve to remind us to pause our week is keeping the Sabbath. This discipline echoes the story of creation in Genesis (2:1–3) where God rested on the seventh day. This is an invitation for us to create a regular day for rest, recreation, and restoration in our relationships and our responsibilities. It reminds us that we are not machines or robots; we are spiritual beings growing into the fullness of our humanity by being aware of our limitations and of our inner lives.

How might you incorporate a regular day of rest and renewal into your hectic schedule?

Reflection Questions

1. What is out of order in my life?
2. What is one change that I can honestly make to bring about a better balance in this part of my life?
3. Do I need a friend or sponsor to help me make this change?

CHAPTER 4

What Is the Meaning of Life?

My friend David loves to playfully tease servers with silly questions. Often after a waiter has carefully outlined all the available meal choices for the day, he will conclude his presentation with the query: "Do you have any questions? David will invariably reply, "Yes. Do you know the meaning of life?"

Mythologist Joseph Campbell responds to the question this way, "People say that what we're seeking is a meaning for life. I don't think that's what we're really seeking. I think what we're seeking is an experience of being alive." This existential yearning is clearly a quest for connection, belonging, or vitality.

This question of the meaning of life usually stumps most of us because it feels so general and large in scope. What if we were to start small and ask, "What is the meaning of my life?" Then we would have something more personal and particular. This perspective helps us to narrow our focus and get real about our interaction with the questions. Good questions help us to go deeper into the essence of the material. For example, this question is deeply significant in that it invites us to reflect on our values, our beliefs, and our aspirations. Rare is the person who can respond to this question quickly and easily. We need time to process all the aspects of that worldview and the ways in which we intend to live out the values we hold dear. This is neither simple nor easy.

As Canadian psychologist Jordan Peterson makes clear, we find meaning in our life by taking responsibility for what is ours to do. This is a very personal decision that unfolds over time. It is not a one-time choice, but rather, a series of choices, leading in the same direction to accomplish our goal. But how do we know what is ours to do?

Here is a story about that quest:

Once upon a time, there lived a king who longed to discover the answers to his persistent questions about life. One day, he called together all the counselors in his kingdom to seek their wisdom. He shared his confusion with them and asked, "What is the right thing to do; when is the right time to do it; and who is the right person to help?" None of them could offer any worthwhile answers.

He had been told, however, about a hermit who lived atop a mountain not too far away. He set off, hoping to seek out enlightenment from this wise man.

He dressed in common clothes but took with him a small retinue of soldiers. At the base of the mountain, he commanded the soldiers to remain there until his return. The disguised king eventually reached the summit, where he encountered an old man digging in his garden. After receiving no answers to his preliminary greetings, he picked up a hoe and began silently working alongside the man. After some time had passed, they were interrupted by the cries of a wounded man nearby. The king immediately went to see how he might help. He tore off some of his own clothing to stem the bleeding. As he attended to the injured man, the king asked him what had happened. The man replied that the king's soldiers had attacked him because they saw him stealthily following the king. "But why were you following me?" the king asked. "I came to kill you in revenge for killing my brother," he said. "But now I see that you are not the bloodthirsty man I thought you were. Please forgive me for trying to harm you." "I do forgive you," responded the king. At that precise moment, the soldiers arrived, and he ordered them to escort the man back down the mountain. He instructed two of them to accompany the injured man back to the palace where he could receive proper medical care.

The king turned to the hermit and said, "Before I go, I have three questions to ask you: What is the right thing to do, when is the right time, and who is the right person to help?" The hermit replied, "I think you have already received your answers. First, when the injured man arrived, you immediately responded by attending to his wounds. Second, you did not delay in meeting your obligation to assist him. Finally, you did not consult me or wait for any of the soldiers to arrive in order to attend to him. Instead, you did the necessary work in the moment in which it was needed. You were the right person in this situation and look what happened—you were reconciled with your enemy!"

Sometimes, asking ourselves too many questions can lead to self-doubt or greater confusion. Deep questions need to percolate for a while to be distilled into more digestible portions in order to be assimilated. This can be done through conversation with others, silence, guided periods of reflection, dream work, prayer, or meditation.

I find that, for myself, I appreciate long periods of reflection and silence as I process questions about the meaning of my life. I have gradually come to believe that I have been created to serve humankind. My "delivery system," as psychologist Bill Plotkin would say, is through the priesthood. This revelation continues to unfold in depth and breadth as I discover the many different possibilities of service to others. The significance of this awareness endures, even when I am very uncomfortable with the choices of service and ministry before me. I know intuitively that this is all a necessary part of my journey toward wholeness. As I lean into my own story, I take heart from the many heroic stories in the Scriptures and cultural folktales. I am encouraged by the wisdom and largeness of spirit of the people who inhabit them. These stories remind me that I am not alone on the journey. I am being guided and encouraged by something and Someone much larger than me.

How about you? What is yours to do? What is guiding you on the quest for your own life? What is your delivery system? How do you tell the story of your life?

David Danby puts it this way, "A story is not a version of life but an interpretation of experience; it is a way of telling, not a way of being, and it reverberates in every direction."

Now, this story from my own life. When I was a very young priest, in my first parish assignment, I was tasked with preparing adults to enter into the Catholic faith. I enjoyed the opportunity to teach and share my learning and understanding of the faith with other adults. One day a middle-aged man asked me to allow him join the class so he could receive the sacraments. Ruben was so touched by his young daughter's conversion experience that he wanted "what she had." And so began his journey of a gradual unfolding of faith. On the day of his baptism, he chose to be baptized during a Sunday service. I was privileged to do the honors of baptizing him in the midst of our faith community. As I began the traditional words of sacramental baptism, "I baptize you in the name of the Father, the Son and of the Holy Spirit," I experienced a sensation so profound that I found myself openly weeping. The tears were tears of joy. In that moment, I came to know my deeper calling, the deepest meaning of my life: I was a spiritual father to this man, and I knew I would be to many others as well. And so it has been, for all the years since that day.

Reflection Questions

1. What gives me purpose or meaning?
2. What fills me with a sense of awe and wonder?
3. In looking back over my life, what am I grateful for having accomplished?

CHAPTER 5

Live to Work or Work to Live?

With the exception of a privileged few, it is the fate—or calling—of human beings to work. Whether in the home, or the office, on the road, or in the uncountable settings of workplaces, we work to sustain ourselves, to put food on the table and a roof over our heads, to provide for our children, and to contribute to the security of our aging years when we can no longer work. In fact, the Scriptures (Gen 2:15) tell us it is part of God's plan for us—it is a means of human fulfillment.

Work that is at least somewhat meaningful and healthy allows us to fulfill our overarching vocation. In his encyclical *Laborem Exercens,* Pope John Paul II reminds us that work is meant to be humanizing in relationship to the world, and it should help continue God's creation in a just and harmonious way.

It is undeniable that many people, for reasons of geography, lack of education, opportunities, or even ability, face limited choices when it comes to finding a job or starting a career. Nevertheless, meaningful work is indeed God's plan and hope for us, so what options are open to us? I firmly believe that the attitude we bring to our work can profoundly affect the level of enjoyment and satisfaction we experience in our day-to-day labor.

There is a well-known story about a construction crew at a building site. A passerby asked a carpenter what he was doing. He replied, "I'm framing this room." She then asked a mason what he was working at. He said, "I'm building this wall." Finally, she asked a young man pushing a wheelbarrow full of dirt, what he was doing. Glowing with pride, the man declared, "I am building a cathedral!"

Can we see that bigger picture? Can we imagine the joy or the benefits we bring to others through our service? Can we see that we are contributing to a worthwhile—even important—cause? Can we fix our eyes not on the wall, but look up occasionally and see the cathedral? Attitude and perspective, whether we realize it or not, play a major role in human fulfillment at work. As Fr. Richard Rohr likes to say: How you do this moment is how you do every moment.

Soulless work can be a tragedy, and can eventually destroy the human spirit. We will spend a great deal of time in our work, so it is important to make careful choices, as far as we are able, in jobs and careers.

So what is our role here in partnering with God?

For many people, getting their first job is akin to a rite of passage. Often this is experienced as a step into adulthood or personal/family responsibility. It is the beginning of a long journey. In the best-case scenario, it invokes an important question, and in these days of multiple careers over a lifetime, the question begs reexamination again and again: What do I really want from my work or career? Here is a short list to help you name more clearly some of your real needs, desires, and priorities:

- Money (of course)
- Companionship
- Personal dignity
- Respect from others for your talents or skills
- A pleasant environment
- Rewards
- A feeling of working with a team for something bigger than yourself
- A sense of accomplishment

- The opportunity to help others
- Regular challenges
- Creative innovations

There is a normal daily tension between work and prayer, action and contemplation. One feeds the other, so we need to be intentional with this interaction. Perhaps this might take the form of dedicating or consecrating your work each day to God. When I use the word *contemplation,* I am speaking of a mindful attentiveness to God's presence. The fruit of this mindful awareness is compassion and justice for yourself and for others. By savoring life, we rediscover God.

However, what happens when you find yourself feeling useless, or unimportant, or outdated? For many of us in middle age, the tech revolution has left us feeling inadequate. Or perhaps you discover yourself not wanting to work anymore, or that the happiness has gone out of your work. What then? It is time for an honest and thorough self-examination. We do this by looking at all the variables of our life and the job. American author and philosopher, Sam Keen, points out, "work without meaning leads to boredom, depression and rust out." Truly a dehumanizing process.

Developing disciplined practices of awareness can lend meaning to our work. Here are some ideas that might be helpful:

- Prayerfully entering the beginning of each day
- Practicing solitude and meditation
- Pausing in the day when possible
- Looking back over the day during a short time of reflection

Some people find it helpful to use symbols or ceremonies to mark parts of their day, whether it be at the beginning of the day or the transition from work to home life. This can be especially suitable for people in high-stress jobs, like healthcare workers or first responders. For example, they might find it helpful to start the day with a positive activity like exercise, reflective reading, or prayer. Others find it helpful to clearly mark the transition into home life from work responsibilities by intentionally changing their clothes, going for a walk, or just resting with a cup of coffee. What works for you?

Life continues to evolve over time; so must we. Albert Camus, French philosopher and author, famously said, "Without work, all life goes rotten; but when work is soulless, life stiffens and dies." What will enliven you or energize you in this important arena of your life?

Here are some areas to explore and reflect on as you seek greater fulfillment in your work. Notice what comes up for you. What keeps you from discovering God in your work? Do you sense any nudges or prompts in a particular direction? Sometimes it helps to talk to a trusted friend or confidante.

Some suggestions:

- Name your expectations
- Know your limitations
- Ask: What do I really need from my work?
- Balance your employment with enjoyable hobbies or volunteer work
- Find a broader arena for meeting your relationship needs
- Practice random acts of kindness toward the newest employee or one who is hurting
- Volunteer for something that energizes you
- Use more humor
- Thank/affirm people who work for you or with you
- Self-check: Has your work become exploitative rather than liberating?

- Treasure rest/leisure
- Another self-check: Has your success at work become a trap?
- Rethink your gifts, skills, and talents
- Make a list of the blessings that work brings you
- Ask yourself: Is it time for a change?
- Focus on the positive aspects of your job and life itself
- Develop an attitude of gratitude
- Actively engage with people who you like and uplift you
- Choose an ethical organization to work for
- Explore in your mind the possibility of working for yourself
- Tap into your imagination (dreams, attractions, yearnings)
- Bring all this reflection to your prayer

A wisdom story: Once a simple cobbler was visited by a wealthy man who wanted to ask him a few questions. "How much money do you make in your work?" asked the rich man. "Well, I don't really know," replied the cobbler. "It depends upon the day or week. I make enough for my wife and I to live a happy, simple life." Despite continued encouragement to give a particular annual amount of income, the cobbler remained uncertain. Finally, the rich man thanked him for his time and then gave him a small sack of gold for his trouble. "I am most grateful for your time and willingness to talk to me. Here is a small gift for you and your wife." The cobbler was flummoxed. He had never seen so much money before in his whole life. The man insisted that he keep the money. When he left, the cobbler shared the good news with his wife and then hid the money underneath their bed. From that day forward, he never left the house for fear that someone might steal the bag of money. Finally, he realized that this was no way to live—in fear. Therefore, he went to the rich man and returned his money. "But why do you not want to keep the money?" asked the man. "Because I prefer my simple life and work, lived in freedom from fear."

This man had confronted that most important question faced by humans: "How do I want to live?"

If it is our faith that sustains and nourishes our life, then instead of leaving our faith at the door, we integrate our faith into our work. This is to live our life from the inside out, rather than the other way around. We call this integrative work—creating our own spirituality. Author Gregory Price puts it this way, "The spirituality of work is a disciplined attempt to align ourselves and our environment with God, and to incarnate God's Spirit in the world through all the effort (paid and unpaid), we exert to make the world a better place, a little closer to the way God would have things."

May it be so!

Reflection Questions

1. How do I feel when I have to get up in the morning and go to work?
2. Does my work or career align with my value system?
3. Does my work engender any joy or satisfaction in me?

CHAPTER 6

Retirement or "Refirement"?

Three priests were enjoying their retirement together in a group home. One morning as they sat appreciating their comradery and morning coffee, one of them spotted a large car pulling into the parking lot. He turned to his friends and said, "Quick, start drooling. The bishop is back looking for us to return to work."

Retirement is often influenced by financial, health, and cultural values. When, where, and how we retire are all personal and familial decisions. Questions that can drive this discussion include:

- Will we have enough money?
- Should we downsize or move?
- What do we have time and energy for?
- What would we really like to do?
- How can we engender meaning in our activities?

As we wade through the necessary challenges and unique concerns of retirement, we will face lingering anxiety. This is normal. Change, planned or unplanned, often brings out varying degrees of anxiety and discomfort. After all, habitual patterns of living are being confronted. As we adapt to new environments, we expand our life experience and grow in different ways. There *is* life after retirement—just not in the way we originally imagined.

For married couples and those in partnerships, this transition can be helped by lengthy conversations about values, dreams, and expectations. Honoring this shift or change in lifestyle through a ritual or ceremony can bring a sacred order to the process. This is not something that we can rush into without creating needless havoc.

Some people will have very limited options while others will have a wide variety of choices to make in regard to their future. For example:

- Caring for ill or aging parents
- Being co-opted by grandchildren (this can be a mixed blessing)
- Realizing that you are in the last third of your life
- Recognizing that you are still very productive in different ways
- Volunteering in your church or local community
- Recognizing that the needs of men and women are different (for example, men need projects, women need companionship)

As you near retirement, do not be surprised if you are drawn to reflect on your unlived life. Are you being encouraged to finish a particular project or goal of yours? Is there something inside you that is inviting you to some new adventure or opportunity? Perhaps you have spent your working life as an engineer and now you are fascinated by artwork; or you have been a homemaker and now you are being invited to get a college degree; or you are drawn to study theology after a lifetime in construction. These intimations are prompts from your interior life. Where is God inviting you to step into the deep? Remember the story of Abraham, who was called in his retirement to a completely new life? He was *re-fired* for a whole new life of adventure.

Retirement or "Refirement"?

There is more to you than you realize. God continues to dream through you. What is God summoning you to do? What are you being re-fired for? Where does your excitement lie? Follow the energy. One friend of mine, a retired psychotherapist, recognized that his new vocation was to create an environment where his friends felt welcomed and could rest awhile from the de-energizing forces of reality. Another person decided to become certified as a spiritual director and gives her time to companion others in their search for God.

Here are some creative ideas:

- Build a legacy for your family by creating a video file for your grandchildren
- Write your memoirs or autobiography (I appreciate that both of my parents did this for our family)
- Share your possessions with your loved ones now rather than leaving them at your death
- Create a dream list of what you would like to do
- Travel to new places—locally, nationally, or internationally
- Be reconciled with your enemies
- Work with the poor or marginalized
- Mentor the young
- Join a group that holds values similar to yours, or create your own group
- Do something different every day
- Participate in cultural events
- Visit museums or art galleries; become a docent
- Improve your computer skills or social media acumen
- Read or listen to books or podcasts that broaden your perspective
- Learn about the other generations

- Care for the planet by picking up litter, reducing your purchases, reusing preowned items, recycling used materials, planting a tree
- Actively participate in bettering the life of others

How do these resonate for you?

Reflection Questions

1. What dreams remain unfulfilled for me?
2. Which tasks need to be addressed?
3. Do I need to make any course corrections?

CHAPTER 7

How Do I Converse with Someone Who Drives Me Nuts?

Some time ago, a friend of mine was greatly distressed about something and wanted to get it off his chest. He said, "You know I hate it when people constantly have to repeat themselves." I nodded, encouraging him to go on. Then *he* repeated himself, "You know I hate it when people constantly repeat themselves." He gave me an example of his frustration and then he did it himself! He never saw the irony in his comments. I kept quiet!

Often what drives us crazy about others says a lot more about us than we would like to admit. Numerous personality tests have been developed to identify our many human idiosyncrasies and similarities. For example, some people are extroverts—they thrive on interaction with others, usually the more the better. Others are introverts and prefer the quieter route. Some people are more concerned with organization and details of an event rather than "going with the flow" of time, space, and spontaneity. Still others are more interested in connecting with people's feelings or relationships. There are some who are vigorously intellectual in discussing politics, world affairs, and environmental issues. There are some who are loud and opinionated and may verge on being bullies; others shy away from any kind of confrontation and difference. Inevitably, these folks end up together in social situations—family gatherings, parties, weddings, funerals, church events, and so on. These groups will never feel comfortable conversing at any length, and yet we are called to recognize every other human being as a child of God, and to accord them respect, courtesy, and kindness. What I do when I find myself in the uncomfortable position of making polite and respectful conversation with someone who brings out instinctive negative feelings in me?

Sometimes the gap can never be bridged. However, in most situations, it is helpful to try to *assume* goodwill on the part of the other, to recognize that they probably have different life experiences, and to accept that they may be having the same difficulty with you and your opinions.

My father and I were on opposite sides of the political spectrum. One day, in the midst of a completely unrelated conversation, he began ranting and raving about the Red Cross. For the life of me, I could not figure out why he was so angry with the Red Cross, of all organizations. "Dad, why are you so upset with the Red Cross?" Pointing his finger at me, to add emphasis to his statement, he exploded, "During World War II, when I was fighting in the Pacific, the Red Cross charged us ten cents for a pack of cigarettes." I innocently asked, "What did you expect them to do?" "They should have given them to us—for FREE! We were fighting for our country." This came from a man who did not believe in welfare for individuals.

Here are some guidelines that have helped me in dealing with difficult people:

- Ask open-ended questions
- Let go of the need to be right or to correct
- Seek to understand the other person's point of view by listening well

- Ask them to illustrate their point with a personal story
- Focus on the real need behind the bombast
- Let go of the need to judge or categorize the other person
- Thank them for sharing their opinion and move the conversation on

Australian author Michael McGirr says that the inability to express oneself is the cornerstone of social alienation. In my experience, it is possible that person is fighting social alienation. Insecure people often try to shout down or overwhelm perceived "enemies." This often comes from toxic shame, which is an internalized sense of feeling bad or unsure about oneself. This can come from the formidable influence of our family or culture in terms of perceptions of beauty, importance, or intelligence. Sometimes an excessive emotional response can be the result of a lack of a considered thinking process. We often experience this in discussions of religion and politics, which show our deepest values.

Confrontational conversation rarely works, but there are exceptions. Even Jesus found himself in one of these situations.

In Mark 7:24–30, Jesus is confronted by a Syro-Phoenician woman who begs him to cure her daughter. It is obvious from the conversation that they are on different wavelengths. He definitively refuses the request because she is not Jewish. He probably didn't expect pushback, but undaunted, she accosts and berates him using a metaphor to challenge his perception and his words of rejection. His response was to graciously acknowledge the truth of her insight and grant her request. We too can be changed if we can move beyond the externals of the situation. Perhaps that is why the Scriptures repeatedly remind us to be compassionate to strangers—that we might be changed in the process—as Jesus was, in this unexpected confrontation. It's worth a try!

Reflection Questions

1. How do I normally deal with difficult personalities? Does it usually work?
2. Can I name a time or two when I have been difficult?
3. What have I learned from people who are different from me?

CHAPTER 8

How Do I Grow Old Gracefully?

Popular American author Mark Twain once quipped, "Out of all the things I have lost, I miss my mind the most." There are lots of jokes and teasing around the aging process—losing our hearing, our keys, our memory, or our vitality. Nevertheless, eventually we all must face the facts of aging in our own way. Will we become like fine wine—distilled and matured by the encounters of life? Or will we become like vinegar—sour and embittered?

We can learn from other elders how to age well and/or how to avoid unhelpful practices or attitudes. One of my older friends taught me to welcome everything, push away nothing. By that, she meant whenever someone asked her to go on a trip or try something new, she always said yes. "It made life more exciting," she said. I am reminded of Fr. Greg Boyle's story about his mother on her deathbed. With great excitement, she exclaimed (in reference to her upcoming death), "I've never done this before." Now *that's* welcoming everything!

Psychologist James Hillman points out that one's character is the active force in the body's aging process. Aging is a revelation of the body's wisdom. As the body ages, the interior life becomes more pronounced. This is one reason why older people tell and retell stories from their past life. They are trying to make sense of the mystery of their life's challenges. Having a sense of the larger myths or stories in life can help us gain insight into our epic struggles, misalliances, and tragedies. What big stories help you to connect your story with something meaningful? Perhaps this might be a story from Scripture, a cultural myth, or a heroic tale.

Mental and physical vitality may decline with age, but our character shows even more energy as our form becomes more actualized. So what do you plan to do with your one wild and precious life (Mary Oliver)?

Renowned Rabbi Zalman Schachter-Shalomi has said that an elder is someone who doesn't just get older, but who gathers up all the pieces of his life and turns them into wisdom. He called this work, harvesting, which involves *appreciating* the contributions you have made through the years, *deciding* what remains unfinished, and *passing on* a legacy for the future. To move from ageing to "sageing," we must pass through the gates of transformation.

What might this process look like? Gerontologist Jane Marie Thibault and retired chaplain and professor Richard L. Morgan have written an insightful book on this very topic, *Pilgrimage into the Last Third of Life: 7 Gateways to Spiritual Growth*. Summarizing their wisdom and experience, they list the following gateways of transformation:

1. Consciously facing the aging and dying process
2. Accepting and living with limitations
3. Doing the necessary inner work
4. Living in and out of community
5. Honest prayer and contemplation
6. Redeeming loss and suffering
7. Leaving a legacy

Aging is a continual becoming and discovery of self, so expect the new and embrace the old. There is no greater gift to the family or faith community than a joy-filled older person. This often includes a healthy sense of humor and laughter. Wisdom and insight come from processing and pondering the lessons of life. It is best distilled through the integrity and self-transcendence of one's life. Old age provides us with the opportunity to develop the richness of who we are. Retired professor Wilkie Au summarizes this work in the following statements:

- To integrate the neglected and underdeveloped parts of our earlier life
- To reconcile ourselves with past regrets and failures and savor our joys and successes
- To root our identity more on internal qualities and values that reflect our spiritual nature
- To live more deeply out of our authentic nature
- To recognize how we can contribute to making life better for others
- To energize our lives with a renewed sense of what gives life meaning

Social activist Maggie Kuhn believed that elders have five roles to play in society as:

1. **Mentors** to teach the young (blessing)
2. **Mediators** to resolve conflict (forgiving)
3. **Monitors** of public bodies (healing)
4. **Mobilizers** of social change (witnessing)
5. **Motivators** of society toward the public good (restoring)

Elders are also Holders of the Tradition, the fundamental values of the ancestors. Wise elders balance traditional understanding with contemporary input. Swiss gerontologist Lars Tornstam developed a theory of positive aging called *gero-transcendence*.

Among many of his insights, he lists the following as most helpful to this positive process:

- A decreased preoccupation with one's body
- Less interest in superficial relationships
- A greater acceptance of ambiguity and tolerance for change
- An increase in one's ability to accept others without judgment
- A greater acceptance of life as mystery
- A decreased fear of death
- A greater appreciation for the ordinary joys of life
- An increased concern for future generations
- A greater sense of oneness with all creation

One sage said it best: At every stage of life we must begin over again. So how will you facilitate your own aging process? Will you grow into your sageness to generate more creative responses to life in general or expand your mythic mode of experience into something much broader?

The choice is yours.

Reflection Questions

1. What am I most anxious about in my own aging process?
2. What am I most grateful for in my life?
3. What wisdom have I accumulated from paying attention to life?

CHAPTER 9

How Do I Pray?

Brazilian novelist Paulo Coelho relates the story of a poor farmer on his way back from the market one evening who found himself without his prayer book. The wheel of his cart had come off right in the middle of the woods and it distressed him that this day should pass without him having said his prayers. This is the prayer he made: "I have done something very foolish, Lord. I came away from home this morning without my prayer book, and my memory is such that I cannot recite a single prayer without it. So this is what I am going to do: I shall recite the alphabet five times very slowly and you, to whom all prayers are known, can put the letters together to form the prayers I can't remember." And the Lord said to his angels, "Of all the prayers I have heard today, this one was undoubtedly the best because it came from a heart that was simple and sincere."

What a creative way to pray! This farmer had learned to pray as he could—with the right attitude.

What an important lesson to remember—pray from your whole self—heart, mind, and body. Prayer is not meant to be done mechanically or by rote, but from the heart.

What is prayer? Edward Farrell in *Prayer Is a Hunger*, says it beautifully: "Prayer is a waiting. It is hunger; it is love. Prayer is a relatedness, and prayer is a stillness....Prayer is a growing; it is a discovering; it is a communion....Prayer, rightly understood, is an expression of the deepest levels of our being."

The whole of the Christian life is about experiencing Christ within us (1 John 5:11–13). Authentic prayer helps us to do this. The very heart of prayer then is seeking God and letting go of fear and anxiety. The purpose of prayer is to become aware of our already present union with God (Heb 10:10). To live out of this union is our task in this life.

Which prayer form(s) will help you do this? In the early church, there were five basic categories of prayer:

- Colloquial or informal (spontaneous)
- Petitionary
- Liturgical or ritualistic
- Meditative or contemplative
- Communion or "feeling"

There are countless prayer forms within and beyond these beginning categories. The key is to pray from your heart. Remember to respect your own personality and the context of your life. What works for one person may not work for everyone. Sometimes we outgrow certain prayer forms as we mature, or the context of life changes for us. Here are three books that could help you get started:

Teresa Blythe, *50 Ways to Pray: Practices from Many Traditions and Times*
Mark Thibodeaux, SJ, *God, I Have Issues: 50 Ways to Pray No Matter How You Feel*
Richard Leonard, SJ, *Why Bother Praying?*

Some signs of fruitful prayer are:

- You present yourself to God as you are
- You have greater kindness, compassion, concern for others

- You have a growing sense of God's personal, faithful love
- You experience continued conversion, change of heart
- You have greater unity, focus, and integration in your life
- You have a growing commitment to social justice and nonviolence
- You have a continuing awareness of God in all events, persons, and creation

Sometimes we can forget that Christian prayer is meant to also include the body. This story reminds us how important it is to listen to the wisdom of the body as one important way of connecting with the Creator.

Several years ago I received a phone call from a hospital requesting that I visit with a woman who seemed to be in some emotional or spiritual pain. As I entered the hospital room, I noticed a middle-aged woman dressed in her blue bathrobe seated on the edge of her bed. She had wrapped her arms around her body and was rhythmically rocking herself back and forth, weeping. I introduced myself and received no reply. So, I sat down near her on the edge of the bed. Then, looking straight ahead, she spoke: "Pastor, do you believe that God only hears the prayers of the righteous?" "No," I said. "I believe that God hears the prayers of any sincere person." "My sister says that God only hears the prayers of the righteous, and I ain't no righteous woman. I've done a lot of bad, bad things in my life." "Do you know what I think?" I said. "I think you don't know how to say the prayers, so your body is praying for you through your tears." She abruptly turned toward me and said, "Do you really believe that?" "Yes, I do. Would you like me to find some words that can speak to your pain?" She silently nodded her assent. We joined our hands in prayer and I said some words that eased her pain. Her crying stopped.

Words and symbolic gestures join to create a holistic expression of our deepest longings. It is then that we feel heard and can find a measure of peace.

What prayer forms work best for you?

Reflection Questions

1. What type of prayer helps me feel close to God?
2. For what aspects of my life am I most grateful?
3. How do I pray when life is difficult?

CHAPTER 10

How Do I Deal with Unanswered Prayers?

Many years ago, my friend Frank Shelley came up with an intriguing idea. He had noticed that numerous participants in his parish prayer group often complained that their prayers were not answered. But that was not his own experience with his prayer. So, he decided to create a "Prayer Exercise" booklet. He arranged the booklet in such a way that the person would write down the date and intention of the prayer and then the date when it was answered. This was meant to give accountability and discipline to one's prayers. It worked! People began to realize that MOST of their prayers had been specifically answered—over 70 percent! His point was that people tend to focus on unanswered prayers rather than the answered ones. This tended to deflate the person's faith. However, as the folks began to use the booklet, their faith in their prayers began to grow.

Of course, many prayers are not answered. Let's face it—we do not know why. Perhaps the prayer is too general (such as "Bless my family") or convoluted (too many details). Or we call on the God of the universe to facilitate a win for our sports team, for weather that will suit our upcoming plans, and of course, for unrealistic things like winning the lottery.

God is not a cosmic bellhop or coffee machine. We don't snap our fingers or push a button and then God answers.

With our friends, we ask and expect them to help us. And most of the time they do. Sometimes they cannot, or will not, for one reason or another. We recognize that prayer is part of an ongoing relationship with God that develops over time. We are to practice becoming better "pray-ers" not to "pray harder" or "in a special way." There are no magic prayers—only people with transformed hearts who pray "in the name of Jesus Christ"—meaning aligning our will with God's will.

The key is the attitude of one's heart, recognizing that the desire for prayer comes from God. God wills this for you, as you will to pray. But despite all this, numerous prayers will go unanswered—for relief from economic woes, for transformation of dysfunctional family situations, for healing of ourselves or others.

What can we do to increase the "success rate" of our prayers? Here are some important traditional bits of wisdom that can help:

- Develop and deepen your relationship with God
- Commit to a daily practice of heartfelt prayer
- Expect your prayers to be answered
- Be specific in your prayer
- Be realistic
- Notice when your prayers are answered
- Give thanks for answered prayer

As you pray, you might consider practicing these traditional steps:

1. Relax physically (take a few deep breaths and focus on your interior life)
2. Speak from the heart (in words, writing, or even tears of frustration or loneliness)
3. Listen and see (open your heart; listen for a prompting or gentle nudge; and pay attention to the details of your life)

4. Respond from the heart and mind (what action will flow from your inner sense or any prompt you receive in your prayer?)

There are numerous prayer forms and practices available. I am sure that you will find a few different prayer forms that will be helpful. How do you discern if a prayer form "works" for you? Here are some questions that can assist you in your discernment:

1. Do you deeply enjoy this type of prayer?
2. Can you be serious about it?
3. Is it a prayer style that opens you to God, others, and all parts of yourself?
4. Can you be original, creative, in your prayer style?
5. Is it a prayer form that helps you take responsibility for your life, letting go of blaming others?
6. Is it a prayer form that facilitates a process of letting go of bitterness, resentment, cynicism, unforgiveness, judgmentalism, and enslavement to memories?

Prayer is a dialogue; it is relational. It is meant to set us free in the awareness and experience of being completely loved and accepted by God. It is a feeling of being deeply comforted and at the same time, of being transformed into our authentic self.

As you journey forward in your prayer life, you will face different obstacles of varying degrees. Remain faithful to the regular practice of your prayer. Pray as you can, not as you cannot.

In times of darkness, desolation, and the dryness of doubt, remember: work against the feeling. Do not allow yourself to be defeated by the desolation; speak with a spiritual director or someone you trust. Connect with your body. This can be simple. For example, although they were speaking in a slightly different context, mystics like Teresa of Avila and John of the Cross would tell people, whether they were experiencing ecstasy or desolation, "Go wash the dishes," or in Teresa's case, the pots and pans. So—pray and persevere, but then go wash the dishes!

Reflection Questions

1. Do I take God for granted?
2. Can I "surrender" my prayer to God and let go of the results?
3. What prayer forms help me sense God's partnership with me?

CHAPTER 11

How Do I Get through Tough Times?

Years ago, a young country boy named Jake was reading and studying the Bible for his Sunday school class. One day the Sunday school teacher gave the class an assignment that was meant to help them in their biblical understanding. However, Jake could not fulfill the assignment, so he asked his mother for help. She was just as perplexed as her son. So, she encouraged him to go talk to Farmer Brown who lived nearby. "He knows the Bible really well. He reads it every day," she said. "I am sure that he will know the answer." When Jake arrived at the farm, Mr. Brown was in the barn working on his tractor. "Can I ask you a question about the Bible?" said Jake. "Sure, what's up?" he replied. After Jake asked his question, Farmer Brown responded with a clear insight into the biblical issue. Jake was impressed. So he asked him a second question: "What's your favorite Bible passage?" Farmer Brown surprised Jake by saying, "It came to pass." "I don't remember that passage." Jake said. "Where is that in the Bible?" Mr. Brown responded, "Oh, it's in many places in the Bible. Son, nothing comes to stay. Everything comes to pass. You remember that!"

Tough times happen to all of us at one time or another. The question is how to face them. What attitude do you bring to bear on the situation? You are stronger, wiser, and more capable than you realize. These difficult times often come to us as a way of enlarging our capacity and helping us to discover that secret which is already deep inside us. We read this truth in Acts 17:28: "In him we live and move and have our being." You are not alone. Christ is with you until the end of time (Matt 28:20b).

Archetypal psychologist James Hillman points out, "The way we imagine our lives is the way we are going to go on living our lives. For the manner in which we tell ourselves about what is going on is the genre through which events become experiences." What if you were to imagine your tough times as an immersion experience or a liminal opportunity where you are on the threshold of revisioning yourself. What then? This change in perspective from the literal to the metaphorical can offer you greater freedom to enter the mystery of the event. Many people experience this truth through games and videos. They learn that these games reflect life—a mixture of skill and luck. We are encouraged by our victories and learn from our losses.

Just like the story, you probably have to search relentlessly until you find the wisdom that will lead you through the darkness of your present challenge. Sometimes others will accompany you in this search. This heroic search will require that you use all you have to face and focus on the task at hand. When you do this work whole-heartedly, you might just discover a treasure inside you that is not only a blessing for you, but also for your community.

Traditionally, a hero or heroine is someone who is well aware of their own weaknesses, but resolves to do the task presented to them, without any fanfare. These people do what is expected of them and more. In the end, their accomplishments are a boon to the community. This cross-cultural model is once again erupting in our consciousness as our society faces overwhelming challenges not seen for a long time. Notice this theme presenting itself through our search for strong (often toxic) political leaders, religious (culture warrior) trailblazers, movie heroes, first responders (raised to heroic status), sports figures (hailed as heroes), and so on. Observe the common thread here: these are *other* people, not us. The invitation is given to each of us: Be your own hero and let go of expecting, waiting, or wanting another person to do the work for you.

On his deathbed, St. Francis of Assisi was asked by one of his young friars, "Please don't die. We need you." To which Francis replied, "I have done what is mine to do; you must do what is yours to do." We each must find our own way to face the tough times that reality presents us. Eddie Jaku, Holocaust survivor, shares how he assiduously worked his way to maintain his mental health and survival: "If I could survive one more day, an hour, a minute, than the pain would end and tomorrow would come."

This is often the underlying reason why people set off on different adventures—to find that treasure.

Anna McNuff, a young British woman, after having graduated from university, was having a tough time adjusting to a career. One day she realized that she was not really living. Gradually a plan formed in her mind of how she could begin to live her life in a more exciting way. Anna decided to ride her bicycle on a wandering route through all fifty states of the USA, covering over 11,000 miles. As she faced untold challenges on her journey, she was rewarded with many "visitations" by helpful people. Her adventure was no less than a journey inward to discover her own description of life and a meaningful career. As Anna says: "When you put yourself 'out there,' way beyond your comfort zone, when you indulge in endeavors that cause your heart to beat fast and your chest to tighten—amazing things happen. Doors open, opportunities arise, and, most importantly, the painful chinks in your armor heal. The cracks that threaten to make you fall apart, they seal over. You become far stronger than you ever imagined." Yes, tough times do come to all of us, but they do not come to stay, they come to strengthen us.

But not everything passes; some tragic situations remain forever. What then?

Reflection Questions

1. What have I learned from tough times in my life?
2. What story, image, or metaphor describes my life?
3. Who are my companions on the inner way?

CHAPTER 12

What Is Joy and Do I Have It?

Many years ago, I had the pleasure of joining several of my friends on a long-distance bicycle ride across the beautiful states of Washington and Idaho. One morning on the trip, after riding for a few days, I was feeling on top of the world. The scenery, the companionship, the camping experience, and the sense of my body feeling fit and exhilarated, all came together for me in a real sense of unexpected joy. I walked over to my companions who were enjoying their morning cup of coffee and said excitedly, "Don't you feel great? Isn't this such a wonderful experience?" They both looked at each other and simultaneously said, "No!" They then proceeded to outline all the things they were struggling with on the trip: their fatigue, the uncertainty of the rest of the journey, and their aches and pains. Obviously, what is good for one person may not be good for others. As I discovered, shared experiences do not always create the equivalent reaction in each person!

Joy is different from happiness. Happiness derives from a moment or passing situation. Joy originates in the soul. Joy is unique to each person; we cannot produce it. For me, joy is feeling absolute connectivity with a person I love, who knows my heart and soul, who will never hurt me intentionally. Joy is a lifting up of our spirits and it brings a smile to our face. I experience joy when I have a sense of at-one-ment with God, or nature, or the cosmos at large. Often this is expressed as a feeling of awe or wonder. It is pure delight.

We often associate joy with children or childlikeness—the ability to enjoy the gift of the moment. Joy is a virtue that is infectious and contagious. Joy is seeing the world with different eyes, without being naive. The joyful person generally assumes that the people he or she meets will be friendly, pleasant, and open to the encounter.

I understand that the word *profane* originally meant *porch* as in the entry point or preparation for the sacred. In other words, all our ordinary encounters are preparations for an encounter with the Sacred. I experience this in my regular morning routine. Perhaps you do as well. This habitual practice of contemplative prayer, spiritual reading, and exercise helps me to embrace whatever comes, even the strange and unfamiliar, not to mention the unwelcome. It gives me a particular mindset that sustains me throughout the day, to be open to the sacred.

I do not want to define joy for you, because you will know it when you experience it. It is unearned and often comes in surprising ways. It has a lot to do with the way you face the world and the people you encounter in your day.

Jesus reminds us that God wants us to be joyful. This is the reason that he came, to show us how to live in love and manifest authentic joy by following his teachings. "If you keep my commands, you will remain in my love, just as I have kept my Father's commands and remain in his love. I have told you this so that my joy may be in you and that your joy may be complete" (John 15:10–11). Joy is an infallible sign of God's presence.

A final story...about fourteen years ago I was visiting a family with whom I am close for a backyard barbeque. The outdoor deck where we were all seated was surrounded by a beautiful subtropical garden, which had an overhead watering system. The afternoon was very warm, so Grandma decided to treat her two grandchildren by inviting them to put on their bathing suits and come out into the backyard, and she turned on the water. I will never forget the squeals of delight and the look of pure joy on the upturned faces of these beautiful children as they stood with the water cascading down on them from above. May you experience the love of God cascading down on you from above and be filled with joy!

Reflection Questions

1. How do I facilitate my own joy?
2. How often do I relive the joyous moments in my life?
3. What lights up my life?

CHAPTER 13

Is That You, God?

God invites us to grow up and mature in our humanity, and we do this best by listening to and collaborating with the Creator.

It is the task of a lifetime, and in the Christian tradition, we call this process "discernment." Discernment is a considered and contemplative process of making decisions that are grounded in a covenant with God in mutual love and fidelity. "It is a continuous succession of choices between two paths, the one leading to fullness of life in the love of God; the other leading in a direction that is ultimately dehumanizing and destructive," says David Lonsdale, SJ. This process is based on the wisdom and practice of the early desert fathers and mothers, and developed further by St. Ignatius of Loyola (1491–1556), who incorporated personal experiences and inner resources in this method.

A couple of stories illustrating what discernment is NOT:

In 1975, my parents wanted to go to Rome as part of a leadership group for the International Congress on the Charismatic Renewal.

The number of airline tickets available to the Los Angeles contingent was limited, but trusting in God's "guidance," my parents went to the airport anyway, believing that there would be space for them. When they arrived, they were informed that there was one no-show, so there was ONE seat available. They discussed their options, but my father really felt that God wanted him to go. Therefore, they decided that my mom would return home, and my dad would go to Rome without her.

As it happened, my dad fell quite ill with the flu after his arrival, and spent most of the time in bed, thus missing the conference.

Was this God directing my father, or was it his own will (and desire) instead? There was no process, and presumably no opportunity to "listen" in a silent space to God's voice. This on-the-fly decision at the airport probably didn't involve proper discernment.

Another story: One day a group of friends went deer hunting in pairs. That night, when the hunt had concluded, one hunter returned alone, staggering under the weight of an eight-point buck. "Where's Harry"? asked one of the others. "Oh, he fainted a couple of miles back on the trail," Harry's partner said. "And you left him lying there all alone and carried the deer back?" "A tough call," said the hunter, "but I figure no one's going to steal Harry."

Not exactly what St. Ignatius had in mind. Moreover, it reminds us of our human tendency to put our needs first and disregard or ignore the needs of others. That can never be God's voice speaking to us.

On the other hand, the more we come to know God through regular and constant prayer, Scripture reading, and an inner sense of being loved by God, the more we will come to know God's will for us in relationship to others. It is a divine relationship that unfolds in time and space through mutuality. Since this is an ongoing journey, we want to work toward letting go of control, sorting out the different voices and letting go of discouragement, selfishness, fear, and misunderstanding. It helps to pay attention to resistances. We come to know God's guidance best by observing the fruits of the Spirit and through our mistakes and successes from previous decisions.

St. Ignatius gave us two words to describe the possible outcomes from the discernment process: consolation and desolation. The experience of these two consequences forms the environment in which we can adequately do this work. Consolation describes a felt sense of interior freedom or harmony with God. Desolation is the experience of a sense of constriction or a dissonance with God. Know your weakness; this is where desolation often strikes. When in doubt, go back to the memory of previous times of consolation.

As we begin this discernment process, it is very important to remember these truths:

- God loves you more than you love yourself
- God desires your happiness and well-being
- God knows best how you will be happy

So relax and trust God. Work for openness and inner freedom; practice loosening the soil of your heart by listening, waiting, in silence. Inner freedom is often translated as unbounded love, deep-seated joy, and endless creative energy.

Seeking your deepest desire is the key to discernment. God's will is in line with that deepest desire. For this reason, we must patiently discern between the many possibilities. Do not rush the process. God's will is for you to be authentically alive, attentive to the needs of others, and mature in your God-given humanity.

Then what are some components of discernment?

- Gathering information about the issue
- Praying silently
- Reflecting on the Scriptures and their principles
- Using your imagination (dreams, nonrational input)

- Writing down the advantages and disadvantages of each choice
- Paying attention to the emotional effects of each advantage or disadvantage
- Noticing your visceral (instinctual) response
- Seeking out the wisdom of mature believers (such as in spiritual direction)
- Reflecting on the events, circumstances, and coincidences of your life

Seek a congruence among these different components. Once you feel that you have made a decision, you might consider asking God to validate or confirm it for you. The response might come in the form of a sign or a particular "visitation" from someone unexpected. This is a way of testing the spirit (1 John 4:1).

I once read about a man who was seeking God's will in his life. He was very new in understanding this process, so he decided to read the Bible for guidance. He did not know where to begin so he decided to open the Bible at random and choose a verse. When he did this, he opened to Matthew 27:5–6: "Flinging the money into the temple, he departed and went off and hanged himself." This frightened the man, so he tried one more time. He then opened to Luke 10:37: "Go and do likewise." As you can imagine, he put down the Bible and did not read it again!

Of course, signs can help us, but even better is a life lived in congruence with God's values and love. After a time of practicing a form of contemplative prayer, reflecting on our life experience, and paying attention to the lessons of reality, we will gradually come to recognize the authentic voice of God and come to know God's will more easily.

Then we will know that we are truly at home with ourselves and with the universe.

Reflection Questions

1. Can I recall a time when I had to make a difficult decision but did not know how to go about the discernment process?
2. What might I do differently now?
3. Is this a process that might be helpful for me across multiple areas of my life?

CHAPTER 14

Where Did I Come From? Where Am I Going?

A woman was once asked by her five-year-old son, "Mom, where did I come from?" The woman thought, "Oh my goodness, this is way too soon to talk to him about the birds and the bees." But she wanted to answer her son's question, so she launched into a short explanation of where babies come from. When she was finished, she hesitantly asked him, "So, does that answer your question?" "Well, not really," he said. "Johnnie told me he came from Cincinnati, and so I wanted to know where I came from."

The landscape in which our early years are lived forms to an extent our identity and our approach to life. In his book *The Solace of the Fierce Landscape*, Belden Lane explains this in several helpful ways. Whether we come from the prairies, cities, the mountains, farms, or a coastal community, we are seeded with a native type of wisdom that is meant to support us as we journey through life. For example, some of my cousins on my mother's side grew up on a dairy farm near Hilmar, California, and they learned early the necessity of long hours, hard work, and responsibility. My siblings and I grew up in a coastal community near Torrance, California. We, too, learned within the family the virtue of hard work, but we also were able to enjoy the outdoor exercise through sports, beach walks, and bicycle riding.

Many people are fascinated by the exploration of their family tree and the tracing of their heritage. Recently this has taken the form of research through DNA testing, which can produce some interesting surprises. For many people, learning that long-held family beliefs about bloodlines are incorrect is very difficult to accept. The urge to know where we came from is the deeper desire to know ourselves better, to create a fuller picture of who we are. We all have a history of one sort or another that is intertwined with family, cultural, ethnic, and national connections. However these connections come to us, there is a lot of chance and happenstance in the mix.

John Donne, the famous English poet, cleric, and scholar, once said that we come from the mind of God and return to the heart of God. This notion of identity is something that can sustain us, especially in difficult times. I know that for myself, this description is very helpful. To know that we are held and sustained by the Creator is a vital lifeline. It certainly encourages us to stay connected in very practical ways, such as through silent prayer, reading Scripture, caring for others, developing a listening heart, and connecting with nature.

To know who we are, to have and to honor self-knowledge, is the beginning of wisdom. This is the first room of the interior castle described by St. Teresa of Avila. We cannot grow in the spiritual life unless we are willing to progress through this first mirrored room of self-knowledge. What caused us to be the way we are? Sometimes it is our genetic makeup, other times it is family dynamics, sometimes it is our choices. Often it is pure chance.

We have an inherent need or desire to know our origin and history. Ultimately it is about our identity and connection with Mystery. How do we know ourselves? Through observation, through our successes and failures, our interpersonal interactions, nature, the arts, and through reading the Scriptures. Not least, we do it through the stories we tell about our life experiences. And we do it without judgment—it is what it is.

So—where am I going? Where is my ultimate destination? We understand that life is a journey, with many twists and turns. We do not always know exactly where we are going, but at least we can gauge the general direction, through the choices we make and the plans that we set out to fulfill.

What do we expect or hope to find "there"? Years ago, when my biking buddy and I were making our way across the northern part of Montana on our cross-country bike trip, we stopped for a rest in a little community called Hope. As we sat on the side of the road, reflecting on the unfolding beauty and challenge of the trip ahead, a young boy came by on his bicycle. He was fascinated by our gear and asked a few questions. So, we asked him, "What's the name of the next town?" "Beyond Hope," he said. Quite a statement about life itself—there is always more in the beyond. For some people, the words *beyond hope* denote despair and negativity, but as Christians, we can trust that beyond hope is confidence in the promise of Jesus that our lives do have a divine destiny.

What do you believe about the afterlife? Many religious leaders use fear and control to keep their followers in line, especially regarding the afterlife. This often takes the form: "If you don't do such and such, you are going to hell." This self-centered perspective takes our focus off God and puts it squarely on us. This, of course, leads to an extremely distorted and fear-filled view of God. From a Christian perspective, we are reminded that we are not to live in fear or be in fear of the future. Instead, we are told by Jesus in his last discourse in the Gospel of John (14:1–21) that he has already prepared a place for us to dwell with him for all eternity. This is Love calling us home to be at peace forever—the Home from which we came and to which we are promised a glorious return.

Reflection Questions

1. What is my image of God?
2. How did my early years of growing up influence my life's journey?
3. What is my image of heaven?

CHAPTER 15

How Do You Grieve the Losses in Your Life?

The story is told about a young mother whose only child died a sudden and unexpected death. Hannah was beside herself with grief; no one could console her, and nothing seemed to help her to process this great loss. One day, Hannah was visited by an older woman who had known her own share of losses in her life. She spoke to the younger woman about how she had coped and moved through the grieving process. She had visited a wise man who was known to have special healing powers, not least of which was that he could read hearts. Immediately, Hannah set out to go and visit this wise man to seek his counsel. When she arrived at his hut, she was graciously received. He listened very carefully to her story of woe and then responded, "I should like to continue this conversation, but you see, I am an old man and it is very cold. I would like to start a fire for the duration of our time together. Would you please go to the neighbors and request some pieces of wood to start the fire?" "Yes, of course, sir," she replied.

"Do not accept any wood from a home that has not known grief." Puzzled by this request, Hannah went on her errand. She went from door to door, but could find no one in that village who had not experienced grief. Determined to fulfil her mission, she moved further afield, to ever more distant villages, but in vain.

Slowly it dawned on her, as she shared and listened to others talk about their own grief in its many forms, that she was not alone—that indeed, grief visits and resides in every human being, every family, every home. Gradually her mourning process evolved, and she could continue living with a measure of gratitude and compassion for others.

Loss sets in motion a train of feelings called *grief* (including guilt, sadness, regret, anger, fear, and loneliness). Grief is our response to loss; it can often be a stripping process. It takes away the sense of safety, security, and comfort that we once knew. In some mysterious way, it initiates us into an underworld experience where we come to know reality from a different perspective. It is not about fixing or changing the situation; rather, it involves humbly facing the weeping mode of being human. Some things can only be known through tears. This loved person or cherished situation is gone—no more to return. The pain thrusts us into the deeper awareness of our fragile humanity and limited nature. It is recognizing that we are invited to love what is mortal and limited, knowing that eventually we will have to let it go. Of course, this is easier said than done.

This process is the mythic path of the Christian teaching as modeled by Jesus. He said it this way: "I came so that they might have life and have it more abundantly" (John 10:10b). This means that he showed us how to embrace and learn from all of reality, not just the pleasant parts. There is no ascension from grief until one has truly received and learned the lessons of the underworld. This is why the various layers of grief are hooked by a symbol, memory, or event. Rollo May puts it insightfully, "All through history it is true that only by going through hell does one have any chance of reaching heaven. The journey through hell is part of the journey that can't be omitted—indeed what one learns in hell is prerequisite to arriving at any good value thereafter."

Grief deepens us; it clears us out. It is a process of letting go and accepting the great truth that every living person or thing eventually ends, leaves us, or dies. Grief places us in a new terrain where several things happen:

1. The pain confronts us with a new and broader perspective and a deeper realization of self
2. In this liminal time and space, the possibility for transformation is created
3. We are moved from loss to release
4. This transitional phase helps us to adjust to a new reality

Often, we can be tempted to ignore the pain of grief by covering it with anger, busyness, overwork, alcohol, drugs, or food. When we deny or run away from this necessary task of facing all our grief, it can, in some extreme cases, lead to psychosomatic illness, depression, bitterness, rage, accidents and/or violence in different forms. John of the Cross said that the language of God is the experience of our lives. If this is so, is it possible that this devastating experience somehow contains God's presence and care for us? If only we can see it.

To leave the place of pain and suffering too soon is to leave the very place of revelation. So stay with the feelings and pay attention to the lesson. This is a highly teachable time—a liminal space and time—where transformation can take place if we are open. There is no predictable time frame or duration for this process. Trust your own inner clock. You know the mourning process is complete when you find yourself saying, "I need to get on with living again."

The four basic tasks of mourning are:

1. To accept the reality of the loss, facing the sense of disbelief and the very real pain of it all
2. To experience the pain of grief, recognizing that there is no right or wrong way to do this, as the pain varies over time and circumstance

3. To adjust to an environment in which the deceased is missing, which includes assimilating new roles and responsibilities
4. To withdraw emotional energy, and reinvest energies into other activities and relationships, learning new skills, developing new interests, and creating space and time for one's self

To go through the process of the stages of grief is to find new reserves of energy, life, and commitment. You cannot fake or rush this process. It is an invitation to encounter the sacred through the wound of loss. As Franciscan Richard Rohr points out, grief is not so much what we do, but rather what is done to us. It is moving from the action mode to the "passion mode." Christians speak of being saved by the Passion of Christ. *Patior* is the Latin verb, meaning "to suffer reality"—to let it work on us instead of us working on it. After a loved one's death, we experience, in some ways, a different universe.

Jesus's metaphor for this work of transformation is the Sign of Jonah. Sooner or later, we all must go into the belly of the whale to really understand this truth, and then to be spit up onto a new shore, a new life perspective. One of the distinct signs or fruits of a well-grieved loss is compassion for others and a deep gratitude for life itself.

What are some losses that can set in motion the train of grief? Here is an extensive list to help you identify and clearly name your own losses.
Loss of:

- Childhood innocence
- Youthful energy or strength
- Health and/or beauty
- Home (moving house, or loss of house through natural disaster)

- Property
- Marriage (divorce)
- Friendship (betrayal)
- Public respect and/or reputation
- Job/income
- Roles
- Loved ones
- Security/safety
- Pet
- Meaning/sense of self
- Church or community as you had known it
- Societal values that you grew up with
- Concept or experience of your marriage or vocation

Midlife presents its own form of limitations as we face the diminishments of our years or realization of the starkness of our reality:

- Unfulfilled dreams
- Lessening of energy, physical strength, or beauty
- Stuckness (marriage, job, mortgage, loneliness)
- Return of the repressed aspects of our adolescent self (impulses, drives, fantasies, and yearnings)
- Is this all there is?
- Existential loneliness
- Now what can I do with what I have?

Another ancillary category is the losses associated with entering retirement. In my experience, this period of life is different for men and women. It seems that men struggle primarily with:

- Physical diminishment
- Meaninglessness

- Loss of direction or purpose
- Lessening of responsibilities

This often leads many men to spend their time in different "distractions" (such as watching TV, online gaming, hobbies, reliving past accomplishments, and so on).

In my many conversations with women in retirement, it is a very different story. For many of them it is a "refirement"—a new commissioning to marshal their time and energy for another focus. This can take the shape of:

- Greater involvement in grandchildren's lives
- More time participating in local parish events
- Return to college or university
- Care for elderly family members
- Developing new hobbies
- Attending special interest classes (like computer skills, art, music)

Let me conclude with a story from my own life. Many years ago, I was gifted with a beautiful Siamese seal point cat that I named Sophia. As you pet owners know, pets have a way of sneaking into your heart, and that is exactly what happened to me. I found myself truly enamored with this beautiful cat. What made the gift even more special was that the parish staff also loved Sophia. Consequently, I had no problem finding a cat sitter when I left for the day or went on vacation. Unfortunately, one day Sophia escaped outside and was hit and killed by a car. I was honestly surprised how deeply I missed her. My priestly theological training did not accommodate funerals for pets, but the parish staff was adamant that Sophia should be duly honored. Theology aside, I finally accepted their pastoral wisdom and prepared a simple service for us. As I reached the end of the service and intoned, "The Lord gives and the Lord takes away. Blessed be the name of the Lord," I wept openly, knowing full well that I was grieving for much more than the death of my cat. I was weeping for all my unacknowledged and ungrieved losses. It is true—life is not fair, but it goes on anyway. To grieve the necessary losses of life helps us to live with a deeper, richer fullness of life. May it be so for you!

Reflection Questions

1. What have I learned from the losses in my own life?
2. What has death taught me?
3. Looking back on my life, what is most important to me?

CHAPTER 16

What about My Marriage?

There was a dying husband who was being cared for at home. One day, he awoke to the delicious aroma of his wife's freshly baked cookies, thinking how thoughtful she was in his dying days. He called out weakly to his wife and asked for some cookies. She did not answer him, so he got out of bed, and in his weakened condition crawled to the kitchen. He called out for her again—no answer. So he maneuvered himself over to the counter where there were several sheets of cookies. He reached up to grab a couple of cookies, and then—whack! His wife slapped him with the spatula and said, "Don't touch those cookies; they're for the funeral!"

We laugh because we know men and women think and perceive differently. It is this difference that reminds us that the work of marriage is about transformation of one another—becoming whole through the discipline of authentic love. The symbol for this endeavor is the crucifix—an ongoing dying and rising to new life.

Much has been written about these differences, so here are some reminders for all of us.

Reminders for Men:

- Women think relationally
- Women listen carefully
- Women read between the lines

- Dates are important to women
- Accept the fact that women are complex and complicated
- Women want words about love, not just actions
- Women need encouragement to feel good about themselves
- Women use language from a feeling base to seek connection
- Women crave emotional security
- Do not leave your wife alone in your marriage; beware of emotional abandonment
- Think connection (reduces fear and shame)

Reminders for Women:

- For men, it's all about respect
- Men are simple creatures
- Men don't read minds
- Avoid shaming or guilting men
- Men are goal-oriented
- Men need to *do something*; give them a job description
- Men need "cave time"
- Don't tell a man what to do; suggest or demonstrate
- Men need routine
- Men use language as a means of sharing ideas

How do we bridge these differences so that we might have more sustainable relationships?

I suggest that you get to know your primary and secondary love language and that of your partner. Regularly practice using this information (see Gary Chapman, *The Five Love Languages*). Ideally, all five love languages enhance a marriage:

- Quality time
- Acts of service
- Words of affirmation
- Meaningful touch
- Gift giving

1. Compassion and understanding are the keys to marriage enrichment. For example, a man thrives on appreciation because it directly nurtures him, while a woman thrives on communication because it nurtures her. The worst thing a man can do is leave his wife emotionally alone in the marriage, while the worst thing a woman can do is shame her husband. Without respect, he reacts; without love, she reacts.
2. Seek the unity of the relationship and happiness will follow.
3. Discover God's place in your relationship and how you deal with mystery. Why is this important? Because this is your operative value system.
4. Conflict resolution is the shadow side of lovemaking. It is passionate and alive for good or ill in every intimate relationship. Here are some aids to help in working through conflicts:
   a. All behavior is needs directed: what need is being unmet or unacknowledged?
   b. Look for patterns of conflict in your marriage
   c. What are your triggers?
   d. Before communicating, think rationally, feel compassionately, and then speak clearly
   e. Move toward forgiveness or letting go of blame
      i. Acknowledge hurt (name)
      ii. Face resentment (tame)

   iii. Choose to forgive (claim)
   iv. Seek reconciliation (aim)
  f. Awareness and reflection are keys to a healing resolution. Awareness (notice and name feelings) + Reflection (process the messages inside the feelings) + Communication (share with the other) will lead to Healing and Understanding
5. Recognize and celebrate each other's gifts and skills
6. Develop a positive sense of humor
7. Practice absolute loyalty to the relationship with no criticism of each other in public
8. One partner may have to do most of the emotional work because they are more resourceful or mature
9. Bring external stimulation into the marriage relationship such as hobbies, career, other relationships, books, travel
10. Meaningful communication
    a. Is it true?
    b. Is it necessary?
    c. Is it loving?
    d. Practice respectful listening and honor silence
    e. Avoid trying to fix the other person
    f. Withhold judgment
    g. Practice appropriate language of apology

A perfect marriage is rare. I always feel a little uneasy when couples say they have never had a cross word in their relationship. This is certainly not the norm. I concede it can happen, but is it something to aspire to? The robust back and forth between two people who respect each other and treat each other as equals can be a healthy and life-giving exercise.

What might a healthy marital spirituality look like? It would include the following aspects:

- Praying together regularly
- Offering ongoing forgiveness
- Sharing life
- Protecting the solitude of one's partner
- Enjoying an embodied presence
- Surrendering into the mystery of the other
- Sharing the cup of gratitude and the bread of tears
- Blessing of others
- Co-creating new life and healing love

In the end, what do you get out of all this work? We all get a healthy and happy marriage that positively affects the communities in which we live and work. We become models of love, acceptance, and respect.

Is this what you aspire to?

Reflection Questions

1. What areas of strength do I see in our marriage or partnership?
2. What do I enjoy most about my spouse or partner?
3. What areas do I need to continue to work on?

CHAPTER 17

Can I Have Fun in My Old Age?

A favorite story in my family is about an old man who was extremely hard of hearing. Finally, after many years of nagging by his wife, he went to an audiologist and got a pair of high-tech hearing aids. After a month of using the hearing aids, he went back to the doctor for a checkup. "How are the new hearing aids working"? asked the doctor. "Excellent! Excellent!" replied the man. "I bet your family must be very happy for you," said the doctor. The man smiled and said, "Oh, I haven't told them yet, and I have changed my will three times already."

We love to tell funny stories and jokes about the quirks and contrariness of older people. Perhaps it is because they no longer have to apologize for their idiosyncrasies. Growing up in the dominant culture of North America, we are indoctrinated into the Protestant work ethic of working hard and taking life seriously. My mother would often tell us in the midst of our relaxation time: "Idle hands are the devil's workshop." This lifetime of over-emphasis on work to the neglect of proper rest and relaxation often does not leave us, even as we age and move into retirement. Many people feel guilty for just enjoying "doing nothing." Others feel that they still must account for every moment in the day. Unfortunately, this often translates into a sense that our worth is found only in what we do, not in who we are. Instead we should find ways to balance out this paradoxical tension between the need to work and the need to honor proper leisure. This is how to lead a virtuous life—living gracefully with paradox and ambiguities.

It can be hoped, as you age, that you have found your spirituality developing in new and surprising ways because of the many gray areas that everyone confronts. Perhaps you have discovered a more abundant sense of gratitude for your life or the gift of humility, or a readiness to forgive more quickly. This is a growth in wisdom and perspective. Holiness is being present to a Presence bigger than you are.

Our beingness itself is very precious (Luke 2:46). Our work is meant to flow from this realization in such a way that our efforts are meant to give us pleasure and enrich the community at large. This is what glorifies the Creator—to live with gratitude and humility and use our work, in any form, for the good of others.

When I refer to "old age," I am speaking of people seventy-five years of age and older. Many authors are now referring to this group as the "Third Age." The number of people that make up this group is increasing, thanks to advances in medical science, better nutrition, and better self-care.

Needless to say, fun is not the same for those in this age group as it would be for twenty-five-year-olds. Our choice of fun activities is dictated by resources, physical abilities and limitations, family responsibilities, energy, and mobility. The loss of a partner is a significant factor here. So much of the context of our life depends not only on what we do to maintain our health and awareness, but also on luck and circumstance. The attitude with which we approach our life can determine the degree of enjoyment and accomplishment. Fun starts with being alive. What is your idea of fun?

My friend Jack is still running marathons at age 76. He calls it his contemplative practice. Another friend, aged 80, is editing books and traveling the world. My Aunt Therese is 96 and still enjoying religious life, after 76 years! But that's not for everybody.

What motivates you? What excites or stimulates you for the day, the week, or the month? Perhaps it is your children or grandchildren, or mentoring younger people, or helping out with the needs of your community or church.

What if you were to view reality as a dropdown menu with a variety of choices? In this way, you could create a schema that could serve you in different scenarios. For example:

- Watching comedies, looking for the humor in life
- Putting pieces together (for example, through puzzles, ideas, crocheting)
- Doing a project (home, community, or church)
- Traveling locally or long distance
- Engaging in armchair adventures
- Looking for and sharing good news
- Mentoring others
- Taking part in celebrations of all sorts
- Facing new challenges with faith, a good sense of humor, and lots of love
- Writing your autobiography for your family
- Developing friendships across generational lines
- Reading or listening to podcasts, YouTube, or TED talks

Recent studies on the plasticity of the brain inform us that change, variety, and diversity encourage the health and growth of the gray matter in our brain. This is significant when you consider what is more important for your life focus: growth or security. Ideally, we want to find the proper balance between these two poles. When we are absorbed with feeling secure, we can find ourselves slipping into a deadening repetition of daily activities, which stunts our growth. Doing things differently can assist in the growth of our brains and keeping our spirit young.

My nieces and nephews nicknamed my father "Grumpy," as in "grumpy old man." He often just sat in his favorite chair reading, waiting for his grandkids to come and visit him. When I encouraged him to practice learning their language of communication (for example, email, texting, Facebook, or Twitter), he demurred. My mother was different. She jumped at the chance to learn this new language so that she could keep the dialogue going with the grandkids. Growth or security? One avenue keeps us open and alive to reaching out; the other direction keeps us locked in comfort and fear of trying anything new.

Which one do you want?

Reflection Questions

1. Where am I engaging life in new ways?
2. How am I poisoning the well of my own happiness (through conversations, attitude, or behavior)?
3. What can I do to connect better with others?

CHAPTER 18

How Do I Accept the Unacceptable?

I met Jose and Maria when, newly ordained, I was assigned to a suburban parish. Theirs is a story of acceptance of the unacceptable—a story of resilience, faith, and determination in the most truly awful of situations. It is a story that stays with me to this day.

Their daughter, Carmelita, at the age of two, needed to visit the doctor for a minor childhood ailment. Tragically, the doctor had not washed his hands before seeing the child. During an eye examination, he accidentally infected Carmelita with something that caused her to become completely incapacitated. For life.

She could not care for herself in any way. Maria and Jose would have to give her constant physical care and nurturing for the rest of her life. As you can imagine, their family and friends encouraged them to pursue legal action so they'd be helped in their intolerable predicament. They refused. They chose to forgive the doctor and move on with their lives. How were they able to move forward? How can any of us move through similar challenges?

To begin with, allow the feelings of disappointment, anger, sadness, and grief to arise from within you. They are messengers from your interior, informing you that you are in a different realm now. This has its own wisdom and way of dealing with impossible messes. Often the most helpful expression in response to the situation is tears. It is a very pertinent reminder to us to practice accepting reality with our whole self—body, mind, and soul.

When we honestly face the very real suffering of "I can't fix this" or "This is beyond me," we then have the possibility of seeing our suffering as connected with the universal suffering of the world. This prevents us from being locked up with self-pity or self-preoccupation, focusing on the need to blame someone or something for our pain. I witnessed this liberating process take place in Jose and Maria. Their suffering softened rather than embittered them. Their compassion grew for others as they realized they were sharing in the very suffering of God and God's creation (Col 1:24). This is a huge mental, spiritual, and emotional leap for most of us, but the image of Jesus on the cross communicates this transforming call to the openhearted Christian believer. This is not about having the pain disappear; rather it is about an interior transformation of perspective. This is one of the core messages of Christianity—accepting and embracing the paradoxes of life.

Thus we begin to accept reality as it moves us to the next step on the journey.

This is easier said than done. It might be helpful to do this in smaller steps, breaking down the painful reality into more digestible portions. I think most people need to process the unacceptable in stages.

Accepting the imperfections of life and/or people is difficult. My brother, Tony, constantly recites the mantra: "It is what it is" to help him in this endeavor. It helps us to observe our self-talk when we face these challenging situations. Otherwise, we can tend to catastrophize the circumstances ("I will never get over this") in such a way that there appears to be no way through the darkness. We need to see reality for what it is, not what we want it to be.

For some people, this breaking down of the experience into manageable portions can be done through the creative arts (art, music, journaling, ritual, poetry, storytelling). For others, this may take the route of supportive friendships, community solidarity, or counseling. Respecting that God is in the midst of all of reality, many people, like Jose and Maria, find that prayer in all its many forms helps them to cope with the ongoing situation.

From the perspective of eternity, the intolerable situations of our lives, unintended and unwanted as they are, can transform us and bring about a broader and deeper maturity in our lives. Often it is only in the darkness that we discover the inner light of our own divinized nature and the power to respond in new and varied ways to life's impossibilities.

Some people find reciting Scripture passages is immensely helpful when facing overwhelming situations. My favorite is: "I have the strength for everything through him who empowers me" (Phil 4:13). I have also discovered that reciting the Serenity Prayer is very helpful in these circumstances: "God, grant me the serenity to accept the things I cannot change, courage to change the things I can, and wisdom to know the difference" (attrib. Reinhold Niebuhr).

The real power of this prayer is that it helps us to face our own limitations as human beings. To move to that place of complete surrender or acceptance of what is, is a very painful but necessary step, if we are to find a measure of peace and integration of the whole of life.

Reflection Questions

1. How do I deal with the unacceptable aspects of my own life?
2. Do I express my feelings honestly and openly to God in these difficult times?
3. Have I noticed myself becoming more mature in accepting the full panorama of life?

CHAPTER 19

Why Does Everyone Have More Money than Me?

American entertainer Jack Benny was famous for his comedic talent. One of his most famous lines about money was framed within the context of a holdup. Jack is approached by a robber who demands, "Your money or your life." Jack does not answer right away. So the robber repeats his demand with more emphasis: "Look, Bud, your money or your life." Jack then muses for a while longer, and then finally says impatiently, "I'm thinking it over."

One of the reasons I want to address this topic of money is that for vast numbers of people this is one of the most anxiety-producing areas of their lives. Let's bring this anxiety to the religious sphere for some guidance or perspective. Can we think about a spirituality of money?

There are a number of levels within the economy, from wealth and financial comfort to financial instability and dire poverty and others in between. I intend to address here primarily financial instability, both real and perceived, with just a glance at poverty. For some people, it is overwhelmingly hard, through no fault of their own, to make a decent living wage—illness, family dysfunction, accidents, lack of education, or circumstances. These can all contribute to financial instability.

Then there are people who really are poor. There can be many reasons for this: family circumstances, miserably low wages, lack of opportunities, indiscreet spending, gambling, loss of a partner, poor investments, and just sheer bad luck. Often injustice is involved. For example, the federal or state government has not provided adequately for their needs. In other cases reckless overspending has brought about ruin. Many people have never been properly taught or mentored in how to adequately make, spend, save, or invest money. They are naïve about money and its inherent power. But almost anyone can learn the necessary discipline if they really want to.

Years ago when my brother, Larry, was working as a financial consultant, he often dealt with clients who believed that they could not make the sacrifices he recommended to improve their financial situation. Larry would then ask them directly, "What do you spend your money on?" They would detail their expenses, and Larry would then point out to them that many of their expenses were frivolous (liquor, cigarettes, fast food, coffee) and could be changed. He was frequently perplexed to hear them say: "No, I need that; I am not willing to give that up." "Not even if it could help you on your way to a debt-free life?" "No," they would reply. "Well, there is the core of your problem. You are not really focused on the goal of your life, nor are you willing to sacrifice for that goal."

This is not rocket science or magic. Although some people are privileged and fortunate enough to inherit wealth, for most of us money is a result of our work. It represents the value that we or others have placed on our work. This value can then be translated into purchases or investments. It takes knowledge, perseverance, discernment, and wisdom to facilitate this. Money is in the service of our decisions.

To clarify, my focus in this chapter is primarily on middle-class people. Usually the wisest course is to work out a reasonable, honest budget and stick to it. This discipline makes it easier to attain financial goals and find a reasonable amount of happiness.

Many years ago, I met with my tax consultant to discuss a way to efficiently manage my finances. During our conversation, he shared some very helpful insights. "Life is difficult for everyone," he said, "How much is enough for you?" "I don't know," I responded. "It's always $10,000.00 more than what you've got. I have worked with very wealthy people and some not so wealthy. They have always given me the same answer," he replied. Obviously, the correct answer is: You have enough when you can let go of your anxiety for the future.

To begin with, we need to develop and nurture a right relationship with money. This is what we would call a spirituality of money—naming our personal value system around money—and what it represents for us. Money cannot buy happiness; but it can assist us in the possibility of being able to do things that we want in our pursuit of living happily *if* we develop a right relationship with money and its symbolic presence. In 1 Timothy 6:10 we read, "For the love of money is the root of all evils, and some people in their desire for it have strayed from the faith and have pierced themselves with many pains." This is why greed is considered one of the seven capital sins.

So it is not the money per se, it is the *love* of money—when we idolize or divinize money to the detriment of proper relationships. This is where proper discipline comes in. We need to strategize our plan and prepare for proper execution of it. There are numerous books on the topic by experts in the field. A good financial planner can also help you in this process. You might look at Dave Ramsey, *The Total Money Makeover: A Proven Plan for Financial Fitness.* His popular book is designed to help people to bring some sanity to financial planning.

Some other insights that can help are:

- Avoid comparing your life to others'
- Avoid unnecessary spending
- Avoid extravagant travel and holidays

- Avoid "can't miss" investments
- Create livable goals
- Put proper value in what is most important to you

Ideally, money should support your value system, not the other way around. Of course, it's okay to pray to God for more money, as for anything else. The real question, from a faith perspective, is will it help others and me, or is it focused just on my own selfish desires.

Is wealth a sign of God's favor? No. It is an indicator of responsibility to share with others, as with all gifts. Unfortunately, many wealthy people have forgotten this part of the equation.

In the end, it is about where our heart is. Probably, we will always feel the need to have more money. It is likely that we will always feel to some extent that others have more money than we do. Ultimately the question Jesus asks us is: Where is your treasure? Does your treasure reside in your heart or in your balance sheet?

A question for all of us.

Reflection Questions

1. Am I comfortable with my relationship with money (income, savings, and investments)?
2. Does my spending honor my value system?
3. Do I share the fruits of my labor and my financial insights with others?

CHAPTER 20

Why Am I Here?

There is a story about a bishop who was visiting a children's mental health facility on All Saints Day. He decided he wanted to talk to the children as a group. So, the staff gathered the children in the main room. The bishop then began his conversation with the question, "Children, do you know why we are here today?" No answer. For some reason he thought that if he repeated the question louder and with more emphasis, the children might respond. Finally, one little boy raised his hand and enthusiastically said, "We're all here because we're not all there."

We are here in this time and space because we are not all there! We are here to work on becoming whole, and we need each other for this process to reach completion.

A Pakistani creation story speaks to this point. The gist of it is that when God created human beings, he noticed that over time they had become violent and disruptive in their interactions. He began to think about the cause of the violence. The more God thought about the problem, the more God realized that something was missing in their creation. And so, he began placing the gift of stories into the minds of all the people. Over time, the violence began to lessen, and people began to be involved in each other's stories.

Psychologist James Hillman has said that because we do not mythologize (tell stories) we tend to pathologize (get sick). Sharing stories with each other connects us and humanizes us. What is missing in you? Where do you need to be more connected to parts of yourself or to others? What stories do you tell about yourself, others, God? What stories touch you and form you?

We are here to uncover what it means to be fully human and so to thrive in our humanity. St. Irenaeus, a second-century Greek bishop, famously said, "The glory of God is man [woman] fully alive." We have been created not just to survive, but to thrive, and thereby glorify God. Jesus said it this way: "I came so that they may have life and have it more abundantly" (John 10:10).

Jesus of Nazareth, a first-century Palestinian Jew, shows us the way. He offers us a recipe or guidebook on how to do this for ourselves. He often told stories (parables) to help us in this work. Like Jesus, we discover the kingdom of God in our midst—where the truth of God and our humanity intersect. Another way to say this is, in the transcendent depths of our humanity, we discover our own inner divinity. This means that in our best moments, we encounter God within us. In our worst moments, God is equally present to love us and forgive us into our authentic nature.

The African catechism poses the perennial question, "Why did God create us?" The answer suggested is insightful: "Because God thought you might like it." We are invited to fully uncover the mystery, gift, or challenge of being in right relationship with all of reality—creation, animals, possessions, or people. Every word we speak, every action we take, changes our environment for better or worse. We can enhance another person's sense of self, we can perfect the environment in which we find ourselves, or we can advocate for the less privileged. It is not about giving money as much as sharing the gift of our authentic presence to make the world a better place. As St. Teresa of Avila, sixteenth-century Carmelite mystic and Doctor of the Church said, "Christ has no body but yours. No hands, no feet on earth but yours. Yours are the eyes through which He looks with compassion on the world...."

We are links in an everlasting chain of being. Life is a series of endless decisions that affects people we encounter and the places that we visit. For this reason, we need to do practical things that God cannot do. As Franciscan author Fr. Richard Rohr says, "Without God we will not do, without us God cannot do."

Let me conclude with this story: There once was a faithful Jew who purchased a residence right next to the synagogue. It needed much attention and repair work. After a time, the owner was pleased by the fruits of his labor. The front garden was especially beautiful. Often as people would pass by the garden, they would complement the owner on the transformation. Many times, they would say, "You and the Creator have done a marvelous job in restoring this garden." He graciously received these compliments, until one day he responded in frustration, "Yes, that may be true, but you should have seen this place before I started working here. God wasn't doing so good by himself."

Reflection Questions

1. What stories do I need to share with others?
2. What is mine to do?
3. Which particular themes in stories do I find most difficult to accept?

CHAPTER 21

How Can I Ever Trust Again?

In 1992, the Archdiocese of Los Angeles sent me to Fordham University for a graduate degree in religion and religious education. It was an incredible experience on many levels. As a bibliophile, I loved the opportunity to buy and read numerous books for my continuing education. At the conclusion of my studies two years later, it was time to go home to Los Angeles, along with my wonderful new library. Now, you should know that I "talk" and "listen" to God in my prayer time, and I sense what God is saying to me in my intuitive function. It has always worked for me that way, and I had learned to trust that voice of love and wisdom.

You may be able to guess what's coming. I sensed that I was not supposed to insure or put a tracer on my boxes of treasured books. So, I "obediently" followed this impulse. Lo and behold, my books never arrived at their intended destination. They vanished and have not been seen since. After thirty years, I think it's safe to say they're gone.

To say that I was disappointed is putting it mildly. I was very angry and resentful. I felt betrayed by God. Several months later, after allowing this resentment to percolate, I sensed God gently but firmly inviting me to look at that anger and honestly address it with him. It was only then that I opened my heart and had a forthright confrontation with God, moving me to a resolution of my conflict and trust in God.

Just as a side note—I now insure or track anything I don't want to lose.

Trust is a moveable feast—greatly affected by life's twists and turns. It is hard won but easily lost. Whether it is trust in life, God, our partner, health, dreams, the church, or the future, we realize that any of these relationships can change overnight. However, in the end, we must all respond to Albert Einstein's fundamental question: "Is the universe friendly?" Your answer to this simple question can change your life and help you to move forward. Do you trust the unfolding mystery of life, your life in all its vagaries? There is a wise saying: "If we knew the journey beforehand, we would learn nothing on the way."

So when we have lost trust in one or more of these aspects of life, what do we do? First we need to look at our alternatives or possibilities. We can become embittered, trapped in feelings of hopelessness, and remain in the past. This leaves us in the unenviable position of repeatedly reliving the past grievance. We become a victim of our own circumstances and pessimistic thinking, which can often negatively affect our physical health. Author Eckhart Tolle says that most of us spend 90 percent of our thinking on negative, repetitive patterns with no real change. Obviously, this does not work very well. It just keeps us distracted.

As we all know only too well, it takes a while to build trust. What is necessary to develop trust? Here are some pointers to get us started:

- Decide consciously to make a particular choice regarding your situation.
- Forgive, that is, let go of the entrapment to the past.

- Walk away from the person, institution, or situation and realize that further involvement is not healthy or helpful for you.
- Learn the necessary lessons from the broken relationship and do not move from the particular pain to a generalized judgment (that is, not everyone will betray you).
- Sit in silence and let all the inner voices be acknowledged. Turn these over to God.
- Consciously attend to the care of your body (exercise, sleep, proper nutrition, massage therapy).
- Realize that some people are simply not trustworthy, especially in certain areas of life (money, the truth, time, promises).
- Move from naïveté to maturity—"Beloved, do not trust every spirit but test the spirits to see whether they belong to God" (1 John 4:1a).
- Surrender to the NOW; this is where all new things happen.
- Let go of the need to control reality and accept life on its own terms.

Many years ago, some good friends ended what had been a long relationship with me. It was devastating, to say the least. I slipped into a lengthy depression and entered therapy to unpack the situation. It was painful but necessary work, to face the loss and its hidden lessons. It took quite a while to find my way onto a new, more mature path in my life. I had to face my own shortcomings in the relationship, my feelings of betrayal, and my unwillingness to trust again. Slowly I began to grow new wings to fly again, trusting in more appropriate ways of relating. I am much happier now. May you experience your own resurrection as well!

Reflection Questions

1. What have I learned from the betrayals in my own life?
2. How is God inviting me to live in the present moment without bitterness?
3. Have I learned to trust in a more mature way?

CHAPTER 22

Must My Kids Be Catholic?

There is an old joke about a woman who died and arrived before St. Peter at the gates of Heaven. St. Peter offered to give her a tour of Heaven and its many rooms. She was delighted to accept the invitation. As they walked down the different corridors, St. Peter pointed out the rooms and their occupants. Here are the Pentecostals shouting and praising God with all their energy; those are the Baptists singing their hearts out, glorifying God; and these are the Presbyterians listening to a lecture about God. Then St. Peter turned to her and said, "We must be quiet now as we pass this room because these are the Catholics. They think they are the only ones here in Heaven."

There is a real danger in religious circles of compartmentalization—putting people into different categories, creating an "us" versus "them" mentality. Jesus is very clear about this practice—don't do it! We are all children of God, brothers and sisters in the *One* family of God.

Another danger is a religious form of materialism that seems to think more is better than less—more prayers, more songs, more retreat experiences, more spiritual reading, and so on. Christianity is actually more about a spirituality of subtraction rather than addition—less religious activity and more practical living out of gospel values.

Parents often confuse faith with their value systems. My question is: What is at the core of our Catholic faith and teaching?

Often we just look at liturgical practice as the essential marker (regular attendance at Eucharist). This misses the point of Jesus's teaching, who put the emphasis on attitudes toward others.

Many young people hold values that are very much in line with the gospel message and therefore with our Catholic faith: social justice, human rights, a commitment to the common good, a living wage for all, respect and inclusivity of all, and care of the planet. All of these are at the heart of Catholic teaching. Think of the papal encyclicals *Rerum Novarum*, *Sollicitudo Rei Socialis*, and *Laudato Si'*. As Catholics, our practice is then celebrated liturgically. It is indisputably true that most young people are missing the *celebration*; but it is equally true that many of us adults are missing the *practice* of these Catholic imperatives. Both are necessary to complete the full picture of the Catholic faith.

Catholicism teaches us that truth, whether it is discovered or revealed, comes to us in different forms. We need to be aware of how God continues to lead us in the way of truth. Therefore, I believe that it is important for us to remember the basic wisdom from the early desert fathers and mothers of the church as to how we can hold together opposites:

- Our thoughts influence our feelings
- Our prayer influences our beliefs
- Our feelings influence our behavior

We are to notice our thoughts and feelings, but not allow them to control us. Rather, it is our silent, openhearted prayer that is meant to guide us and strengthen us on the way of the Lord.

Of course, there is a sense of loss, sadness, and failure about the next generation, more specifically, if your children are not fully participating in your Catholic faith. Often this sadness is also connected to the ending of a family "tradition" of sorts. I know that I have had to go through this grieving as well, in connection with several members of my own family's next generation.

Remember, they are growing into their own adulthood, making choices, trying new ways of being human, and facing their own challenges in this ever-evolving world of ours. We trust that God will direct them, as God has directed you, in this life. Will your children be doomed if they do not go to Eucharist? NO! In Matthew 7:21 we read, "Not everyone who says to me, 'Lord, Lord,' will enter the kingdom of heaven, but only the one who does the will of my Father in heaven."

Every person must make their own decisions in life. We cannot force them one way or another. We can only invite them and model for them practices that bear the fruit of kindness, gentleness, forgiveness, listening hearts, and hospitality. We are told very clearly, "Stop judging, that you may not be judged" (Matt 7:1). Judgmentalism has no place in the Christian way of life. Instead, focus on the common values that you share with your children.

Being Catholic or not is not God's criteria, it is how we live our life. God does not have a checklist, even given the dramatic language attributed to Jesus in Matthew 25:31–46. God's ways are far above our own limited ways of seeing things, especially when it is a matter of seeing into the human heart.

There is another old joke told about a man who died and stood before St. Peter at the heavenly gates. St. Peter said compassionately, "Sorry, but I do not find your name here in the Book of Life." "How is that possible?" asked the man, "I have been a good person." St. Peter then explained that entrance to Heaven was done via a numbers system. One accumulates a certain number of points for certain specific actions. You need one thousand points for entrance. "So what have you done to deserve Heaven," he asked. The man replied, "I have been faithfully married to the same woman for 36 years." "Wonderful! That's worth 35 points."

And so the man continued to list all his good deeds—serving as a lector, eucharistic minister, member of a prayer group, charitable giver, and more. "How many points is that?" he asked. "I am sorry to tell you, but that comes to just 110 points" "Is that all? Oh, St. Peter, please have mercy on me and let me in. I know that I am not worthy." Peter said, "Congratulations, brother. That request for mercy is worth 890 points. Welcome!"

God is mercy within mercy.

Reflection Questions

1. What am I doing to help my children feel more welcome in my religious sphere?
2. How do I demonstrate the gospel attitudes of compassion, kindness, and acceptance of others?
3. Where is God inviting me to reach out in different ways to others, to find common ground?

CHAPTER 23

Have You Ever Actually Met God?

A young blind boy was selling apples on a street corner. One day, in the crowded afternoon rush, a businessman hurriedly walking by accidentally knocked over the boy's small cart of apples, sending them all over the sidewalk. With a quick apology, the businessman hastened on his way. However, a woman passerby noticed the encounter, went over, and began to help the upset boy gather the apples. After the task was completed, the boy innocently asked the helper, "Are you God?"

We naturally associate compassion, mercy, and kindness with God and with God's friends. I now invite you to pause and think for a moment, about some Christians that you know of who have seemingly met Christ, but are violent (in attitude, words, or deeds), creating disunity and disharmony in family, community, and nation. I am not referring to those missteps that can happen to any of us. I am alluding to the regular attitudes, words, and deeds that form a person's life. This is not in line with the God of the scriptures nor the proclamations of the prophets. Misalignment of this sort seriously damages the understanding of what it means to be a follower of Jesus. To be a disciple of Christ is to be like the Master in attitude, words, and deeds—no excuses!

I loved my late father dearly. He spoke to God as an old friend, and he also constantly told us that God had given him a particular message about this or that matter at hand. None of us in the family had any doubt that Dad had "met God." One evening, when we were on our way to a restaurant, Dad recounted with great joy and delight the men's retreat he had just completed. "I never realized all men are my brothers," he said. "I feel like I am loving my brothers for the first time." Later in the evening, as we neared the end of our dinner, a discussion arose about immigration and undocumented persons. "I know what I would do," roared my father, "I would machine gun the whole lot of them at the border." The irony of his words was lost on him. Had my father *actually* met God? Maybe, but I suspect he was not listening to God's side of the conversation.

Let us be clear—God is not like us. God does not necessarily share our opinions or ideas, no matter how good they may appear to be. Sadly, this disconnect from God and from the scriptural values of our faith is not unusual for many well-meaning religious people. Unawareness or disconnection is one of the many obstacles that prevent us from moving forward in living out the values of the kingdom of God.

People like my father have a difficult time holding the paradoxes of life together. Politics and religion get all mixed up. Then God gets lost in the melee and is forced to take a back seat.

Reality is a lifelong journey of conversion from our own favorite repetitive thoughts, beliefs, and behaviors. Think of the number of times that Jesus was "converted" through his interactions with non-Jews such as the Samaritan woman, the Roman centurion, the Syro-Phoenician woman, or the Gentile demoniac. Jesus slowly came to realize that his mission was to all people, and not just to Jews. However, it was sometimes painful for him; he did not fit in with the crowd.

God delights in diversity. Perhaps this is why God created over 300 different classes of beetles. We can learn from this abundant generosity of the Creator by humbly recognizing that there is no one way to be human. God looks to us to creatively live our dissimilar lives with a real openness to forming a unitive whole.

Like Jesus, we too grow into our own humanity, sometimes at a slow pace. People who have truly met God exhibit a large heartedness, a deep compassion for others, a generosity of service to those in need; they are filled with gratitude and live with a reverence for creation. These individuals can handle the kind of paradox that landed my father in trouble.

St. Augustine of Hippo (AD 354–430), theologian and philosopher, recognized that there is no such thing as a onetime conversion experience that covers all aspects of our humanity. He spoke about varying degrees of conversion or deepening modes of maturity in all the aspects of our humanity:

- Theological
- Relational
- Institutional
- Intellectual
- Emotional

If we are serious about growing in wholeness (Eph 4:13–16), we each must be willing to embrace this ongoing task of being converted in grace, through reality itself. This is God's most helpful implement. For this reason, we are to choose our regular practices carefully. You will know you have met God when:

- You know experientially that you are completely loved and forgiven
- You see yourself as belonging to all of creation and part of the larger whole
- You experience yourself in communion with all that is, and therefore live in peace and harmony
- You regularly give yourself in reverence and compassion to others in need

- You live your life in humility and gratitude
- You experience the fruits of the Spirit growing through you
- You live grounded in the present moment, aware that you are God's presence here on earth

These are the kinds of people that we should listen to, not the loudest, nor the most well connected, or the most pious. These are the folks who have *actually* met God. We call them saints. Saints are those individuals who live their lives authentically as the very light of God here on earth.

Reflection Questions

1. Where have I met God in my life?
2. Where do I need to allow God's love to convert me to God's perspective on reality?
3. How am I being God's presence here on earth?

CHAPTER 24

Am I My Brother's/Sister's Keeper?

There is a very touching wartime story of a Vietnamese boy who was asked by medical professionals to donate blood for his little sister who was badly injured. After giving it some thought, he consented. Once the two siblings were connected for the procedure, the boy began to cry. The nurse checked to make sure he was not in pain and then called for a translator to find out what was troubling the boy. The translator turned to the nurse and said the boy wanted to know when he was going to die. It turned out that he thought he was giving his life for his sister. It took a while for the adults to explain that he was only giving one pint of his blood to help his sister, not all his blood.

Quite an extreme example of Jesus's words: "Unless a grain of wheat falls to the ground and dies, it remains just a grain of wheat; but if it dies, it produces much fruit" (John 12:24). The boy knew instinctively that he was connected to his sister and must offer this gift as part of his relationship to her. This is the core message of Jesus: we are all connected and belong to each other.

Human societies can only thrive when there is justice and a measure of equality among their members, and they will flourish to the extent that such equality exists. This will invariably involve a sense of mutuality and reciprocity. With humans being as they are, there will never be a perfect and just society, but we are talking about degrees of health of community.

The more social justice flows through the system, the happier and healthier everyone is. It is very difficult, if not impossible, for government to attain this ideal alone; it always requires the will and generosity of the people as well, to look after the poorest and most vulnerable in society. This will not happen automatically. It takes commitment, work, determination, and vision to achieve the goal of a fair and just society.

In the Scandinavian countries, the lives of all the community members are well protected and enhanced through the willingness of the general populace to share the burdens, the costs, and the benefits of living in society. This is our Christian call to live an authentic community where all members are cared for in a just manner.

Catholic social doctrine has been called by many people "the great secret of Catholic teaching." Here are some key building blocks of this teaching:

1. Human dignity
2. Respect for human life from womb to tomb
3. Peace and disarmament
4. Full participation in society
5. Preferential option for the poor and vulnerable
6. Global solidarity and development
7. Stewardship of creation
8. Subsidiarity
9. Human equality
10. Community and the common good

Jesuit William J. Byron comments: "Principles, once internalized, lead to something. They prompt activity, impel motion, direct choices. A principled person always has a place to stand, knows where he or she is coming from and likely to end up. Principles always lead the person who possesses them somewhere, for some purpose, to do something, or choose not to." Matthew 25:31–46 makes it clear that it is the poor and marginalized who will be our final judges. In addition, the poor and rejected ones clearly portray our real faith and religion. Archbishop Hélder Câmara of Brazil, famously said, "As long as I fed the poor, I was called a saint. However, when I began to ask why are these people poor, I was called a communist."

This is much, much more than making donations to our favorite charities. It is about becoming the reality that we proclaim in our Scriptures, our creeds, our liturgies, and our faith. We are to become the very compassion of God on the face of the Earth. U.S. Cardinal Joseph Bernardin often noted that we must look at life as a seamless garment from womb to tomb, protecting it for ourselves and for others.

A story: Once a young man was walking along a riverbank on a warm spring day. As he walked, he heard a cry for help from a man thrashing around in the river. Seeing no one else around, he took off his shirt and shoes and jumped in to save him. After the rescue, he put his clothes back on and continued his journey. Soon there was another cry for help from a woman who was struggling to make it to shore. He rescued her as well. By now there was a small crowd cheering him on and welcoming the woman to shore. After this second rescue, he dressed himself, and headed up stream just as he and the crowd noticed a boy drowning in the current. People pointed to the boy and asked the man, "Aren't you going to save him? Where are you going?" He said, "No. You save him. I'm going upstream to find out who keeps throwing these people in the river."

This story reminds us of the three traditional levels of care, responsibility, and obligation that are clearly ours to honor in our relationship to our brothers and sisters (direct aid, skills training, and social advocacy). This is poignantly reflected in the Good Samaritan story (Luke 10:25–37) where the focus is not just on the rescue, but on the assumption of care and responsibility for the fundamental needs of the victim.

An undeniable challenge for every Christian.

Reflection Questions

1. What do I regularly do to remind myself of my connection to others?
2. How do I interact with or care for the poor or marginalized?
3. How is God inviting me to expand my circles of concern?

CHAPTER 25

What Makes You Happy?

On the evening of March 24, 1975, Alex Mitchell was sitting in his living room, watching his favorite TV show, *The Goodies,* a raw and physically humorous sitcom. After watching a particularly funny slapstick segment of the show, Alex could not stop guffawing at the antics of the two actors. After a prolonged bout of nonstop laughter, he slid off the couch, having suffered a fatal heart attack. His widow eventually wrote *The Goodies* a letter, thanking them for making her husband's last moments so enjoyable.

What makes you laugh so heartily, enjoy something so intensely, or feel so connected? Each of us has a happiness quotient. How are you filling up your quota for the day? So often we expect or depend upon others to make us happy. I know of one woman who left her husband because he did not do this for her! She was unwilling or unable to find the resources within herself to enjoy life and expected him to fill the void.

Let me be very clear: We are each *responsible* for our own happiness. Happiness is an inside job. It is a direct result of how you interpret a specific situation. A good example of this truth will often be apparent in your own original family. As siblings, you each grew up in the same or similar environments. The way you judge this experience will be unique to each of you. The filters through which you choose to "see" the childhood or adolescent environment will enhance or cripple your view of yourself, the family, and life itself. In many ways, your choice will determine your happiness quotient. We are not pessimists by birth. We *learn* to distrust reality. We must work at being happy.

Here's an amazing story from Eddie Jaku's memoir, *The Happiest Man on Earth*:

Eddie was a Holocaust survivor who was interned in Auschwitz. He grew up in a very loving, supportive Jewish family in Leipzig, eastern Germany. His patriotic love for Germany completely disappeared on *Kristallnacht*, when he was beaten half to death by Nazi soldiers and witnessed the senseless destruction of his home and his neighborhood. His imprisonment in Buchenwald only served to drive this awareness deeper into his brain—that he was a prisoner in his own country, his only offense being that he was Jewish by birth. His story involves a series of escapes, coincidences, recaptures, and torturous beatings. Importantly for him, his skills and knowledge were recognized by his captors, and he was put to work for the Nazis as an engineer/mechanic. In Auschwitz, Eddie lost everything: his family, his possessions, his dignity, and his faith in humankind. This cruel fate, however, taught him many important lessons, and they are the very lessons we ourselves might take to heart:

- One step at a time
- Friendship heals and strengthens us
- A good education is a lifesaver (he was a precision engineer)
- You can find kindness anywhere
- If you lose your morals you lose yourself
- Where there is life, there is hope, and there are always miracles in the world even when all seems dark

and finally

- Love is the best medicine for healing our pain

At his very lowest point, near the end of the war, Eddie was deathly ill with cholera and typhoid, and severely malnourished, weighing only 62 pounds, with a 35% chance of living. At that point, he made a promise to God that if God saved him, he would live his life with an entirely different attitude: he would live every day to the fullest and be an instrument of healing and reconciliation to counteract the atrocities of the Nazis. In his own words, Eddie shares his recipe for happiness: "You have to try to be happy with what you've got. Life is wonderful if you're happy....Happiness doesn't fall from the sky; it's in your hands. Happiness comes from inside yourself and from the people you love. And if you're healthy and happy, you are a millionaire."

Eddie learned a priceless lesson from the pit of human despair: if you do not transform your pain, you will pass it on. It was hard work, but he did it. He transformed his suffering, and the wounds became sacred for him and for the others with whom he interacted. What a witness to the power of a changed attitude!

After the war, Eddie lived a long, happy, and fulfilled life in Australia, dying in Sydney in 2021, aged 101, surrounded by his loving children and grandchildren.

What can we learn from Eddie's wisdom? Happiness is an attitude that flows from the discipline of your vision or perception of reality. Do you live your life as a victim or as an active participant in creating your own story? Many people find it helpful to live each day by centering on what they are grateful for. Others discover that focusing on the good, the true, and the beautiful sustains them. For many others, it is avoiding as much negative news or toxic people as possible. Finally, numerous people have found that actively managing their health—exercising, eating nutritious meals, interacting with other healthy people—greatly improves their happiness quotient. What works for you?

As psychiatrist Victor Frankl has pointed out, we discover meaning through work, suffering, and love. It is not free; it is a hard-fought struggle. Think of how a diamond is formed—

through intense heat and pressure. We are all diamonds in the rough, battling with varieties of stress and pressure points. What attitude do you bring to your work, suffering and relationships? Can you see yourself as a cocreator or adventurer in the crafting of your life? You are not alone in this effort. There are helpers, often hidden, along the way who are waiting for you.

St. Paul in his letter to the Philippians (4:4–7) gives us some very practical wisdom:

> Rejoice in the Lord always. I shall say it again: rejoice! Your kindness should be known to all. The Lord is near. Have no anxiety at all, but in everything, by prayer and petition, with thanksgiving, make your requests known to God. Then the peace of God that surpasses all understanding will guard your hearts and minds in Christ Jesus.

There was a woman who worried about many things in her life—her husband, children, possessions, and her future. She yearned to find release from the chains of her worry. So she set out from her village seeking the wisdom that eluded her. One day, she came upon a beggar who seemed strangely content and even happy. She began a conversation with him and asked him directly, "How have you come to such happiness?" He replied, "One day I finally realized that most of my worries never came to pass. That day I vowed to live each day as if it were my last day and the only day of my life. This awareness has given me such joy." May you experience such happiness in your life!

Reflection Questions

1. What gives me delight?
2. How have I experienced happiness?
3. What do I need to do to become happier?

CHAPTER 26

Communion: Really?

How would *you* describe the experience of "communion"? Let me give you two stories to open a door to this discussion. They are both stories about family: one is my own and the other is that of a close friend.

For over thirty years, my brothers, Tony, Daniel, John, and I have regularly gathered for several weekends a year. We enjoy each other's company, and we spend our time catching up on each other's lives, playing games, and going for walks, as well as wrestling with the deeper issues of life. Over time, this has led us into some very vulnerable sharing and intimate experiences. Each of us in our own way has voiced our gratitude for our time together and the experience of deep connection and belonging. Admittedly, this has taken commitment, choice, and ongoing reflection, but these are very real experiences of communion for us.

Recently, I attended a lunch for a dear friend given by her two brothers and their wives to celebrate her eightieth birthday. This family is not naturally inclined to intimacy or addressing the real questions of life. I knew Louise had long held questions about aspects of the family's history. There were secrets, question marks about illegitimacy in previous generations, but these things were never talked about. Over a few glasses of wine and an excellent meal, very gradually the conversation opened up. And I watched as three normally introverted, reserved siblings ventured into territory they had been unwilling or unable to explore before. Over four or five hours, the conversation became more and more animated, affectionate, and peppered with laughter. Something opened, and something connected. That night and the next day, unusually for this family, numerous texts and emails flew back and forth. Trust, openness, and affection filled the air. Communion had been established.

Communion is hard won. It involves mutuality, reciprocity, and trust. It rarely just happens.

What about the liturgical action we Catholics call "holy communion?" In a sense, all communion, just by its unitive nature, is holy, but what of the communion we celebrate in the Eucharist? We read of the great saints' ecstatic experiences of receiving communion, and yes, in these elevated lives, it does happen. Their experiences are grounded in very disciplined lives of prayer and good works. But what about us? How is it possible for us to experience more than liturgical communion in the Eucharist?

We go to Eucharist to receive communion to remember who we are, where we fit in relation to God, others, creation, and history. Some people treat this liturgical action as if it is magic. However, it takes discipline to make this happen: choices, commitment, openness, trust, ongoing reflection. God will do God's part in this exchange; we must do our part. This is the authentic work of liturgy—paying attention to what communion really means—connection and belonging. This is the core of the liturgical experience—gathering as a community. From this communion flows the responsibility to share the fruits of the unitive experience with others in compassion, service, forgiveness, and affirmation.

Another way to express this mystery is to remind ourselves that we are already in communion with God and the world around us. In the Gospel of John (15:1–10), we are given a wonderful parable of this connectedness—the vine and the branches. Jesus says that he is the vine, God is the vine grower, and we are the branches. As long as we remain in this relationship, we are in love and in union. When we do something that is unloving, at that moment we are out of union. This can be in the form of thoughts, attitudes, or behavior. That is why Jesus says, "Remain in me, as I remain in you" (John 15:4). We cannot do this work without God.

When we are not "in communion," it can be a hellish experience, a source of alienation and isolation. This is where the concept of original sin or separateness came from—being out of right relationship.

All the sacraments point to this reality—that we are already in communion with God. It is not so much that we receive grace through the sacraments; rather we receive the sacraments to remind us that we are already graced. We tend to come to this truth through our own human experiences rather than through intellectual reasoning. We share in the light and the dark, the pain and the joy of humanity, whether alone or with others.

We could also use the words *connection* or *belonging* to remind us of this innate truth. Its opposite, of course, would be separateness or deep loneliness. Here, I am using human language, rather than churchy or philosophical language.

Some people experience this connection through friendship, creation, music, art, or perhaps even a community event. I have heard people speak of concerts, sporting events, or particular religious conferences as being occasions of deep connection or belonging.

For myself, I have often found this spirit of communion or connection in nature. One memory that particularly stands out for me is the time I spent five weeks hiking and kayaking with a group of adventurers in Alaska in the Brooks Range area above the Arctic Circle. During this time we saw only six other people. We were completely immersed in nature in a way that I had never experienced before, and I sensed a real connection with the Creator and with the wildness and beauty of my surroundings.

But after five weeks, I was hungering for Eucharist; I knew that the communion I was experiencing was intimately linked with its liturgical expression. On the last day of the trip, I was able to attend Sunday Eucharist with one of my fellow travelers at the tiny local church in Kotzebue. As we entered the church, we were greeted warmly by the local Inuit community. We had not showered for five weeks, so we stood somewhat apart, at the back wall. At the sign of peace, we were profoundly moved when the whole community came and offered us peace. When we received the Eucharist, it was an exclamation point to the many communions that we had already "received" in nature, through each other, and as strangers coming into this community of faith.

At the Last Supper Jesus said, "Do this in memory of me" (Luke 22:19). Every time we create communion or receive communion, we are remembering Christ and his teachings, not in a nostalgic way but with an active engagement.

At home, at work, at play, in every facet of our lives, Christ invites us to "Go and do likewise." That's Communion—Really!

Reflection Questions

1. When have I had experiences of connection or communion with others?
2. What specific experiences with creation have deepened my sense of belonging?
3. Have my God experiences reminded me of my innate connection to God?

CHAPTER 27

We Know What We Are Against, but What Are We For?

What is it like for you to be a Catholic? Is it joyful, energizing, fun, inspiring? Or is it a matter of following a bunch of rules, having a sense of security, being right, having all the answers, or, worse still, allowing guilt to impair your life? Do you feel like you belong to the "Sunday Comfort Club" or are you making a difference in your own and other people's lives? Spirituality is not a compendium of laws to be obeyed, but an engagement with a Presence to be seized, undergone, and enfleshed.

Often we are given the bad news first—all the do's and don'ts—rather than being introduced into a vibrant relationship with the living God. In this scenario, we miss the power of God's life changing love. Remember, first comes mysticism (the experience) then morality (the response to the experience) and then right behavior.

Many years ago, I had a wonderful opportunity to join a group of adventuresome adults on a backpacking and kayaking trip to the Brooks Range area of Alaska for five weeks (already mentioned in the previous chapter). We all came from different backgrounds in life. Several of my companions were fascinated by the fact that I was a priest, and so asked me numerous questions about Catholicism and the church. Susan, a Baptist in her upbringing, was especially interested in my reflections on our approach to Christianity. I remember one of her many questions: "How come you Catholics get to dance, smoke, drink, and go to movies with impunity?" she asked. I said, "Maybe it's because for you Baptists, if something is not specifically endorsed in the Bible, you are not allowed to do it. For Catholics, if it is not mentioned in the Bible, we can pretty much do it in moderation." Some months after I returned home, I received a phone call from one of the adventurers who informed me that Susan was taking classes to become a Catholic. What happened? Susan gradually realized that her values and experience of reality aligned more with the Catholic vision, and so decided to affirm that awareness by becoming Catholic.

Many authors have written extensively about the philosophical, theological, scriptural, and liturgical details of the Catholic faith. Here I would like to offer you a very condensed positive version of Catholicism to get us started. We believe in these key themes:

1. We have a sacramental world view
    - There are vestiges of God everywhere (look at creation and reality)
    - We are sacrament in the world and to the world (following Jesus and his example)
    - We are to enjoy everything in moderation
2. We affirm a strong connection between nature and grace
    - Grace builds on nature and perfects it, transfigures it (God works with what is)
    - We hold a consistent life ethic—from womb to tomb (God is present in all of life)

   - We honor the sacredness of human sexuality (we share in God's nature of self-communication)
3. We believe in the strong connection between living and dead
   - Communion of saints (we are connected to those who have gone before us)
4. We enjoy the superabundance of mercy
   - There's always room for everyone (we are each unique expressions of God's life in the world)
   - Life is a process of conversion, healing, and growth (reality is God's invitation to continue to learn and grow)
   - God is always ready to accept us back (mercy extends even beyond this life)
5. We live in a profound grayness—a mixture of glory and grime
   - Faith and doubt, grace and sin, laws and freedom, hope and despair (God works in a multidimensional way bringing it all together)
   - We respect human knowledge seeking understanding (we believe in revelation as well as the ongoing discovery of God's truth)
6. Our Faith is inclusive
   - It is not confined to one culture or perspective (universal expression of God's love of humanity)
   - Every aspect/dimension of our lives has importance (God works with the larger vision of life as well as the details of life)
   - All religious experience is mediated through culture in a particular time and place
7. We seek social transformation
   - The gospel message is meant to be shared at every level of human life—personal, communal, national, universal

- To better the human condition, we work for the transformation of unjust structures (the principle of human equality)
- We are concerned for human betterment—justice and peace (the principle of human dignity)
- We are committed to care for human life from womb to tomb
- We are faithful stewards of creation

8. All the baptized are called to fullness of life in Christ
   - The call to holiness is universal (living our life to the fullest)
   - We must live lives of enlightenment and integration (recognizing that we are all connected)
9. Life is to be lived out in community
   - It's not all about you (we are stewards in service to others)
   - We are formed in Christ through relationships (it is love that changes us)
   - We belong to each other (we are God's family)
   - We celebrate our diversity (God's presence is expressed in countless ways)
10. We are a biblical people
    - The Scriptures are the basis for prayer, worship, sacrament, morality (summary of our religion)
    - All truth comes from God whether revealed or discovered (God is immersed in all that is)
    - We have a profound sense of history and tradition (we are a part of a long line of creation)
11. We are a liturgical community
    - Catholic life is rooted in and flourishes in the Eucharist (the summary experience)

- Our tradition emphasizes both the communal and personal aspect of prayer (we are in this together)

12. The Trinity is the centerpiece of Catholic spirituality
    - Cultivating, sustaining, building, and nurturing relationships that are equal, mutual, and reciprocal is the way we mirror the Divine life
13. The Incarnation is both gift and responsibility
    - We find and are found by God in a particular time and place (the present moment is God's space)
    - We are God's beloved children (nothing can separate us from God's love)
    - We are instruments of blessing, healing, nourishment, forgiveness to others (we are God's presence on earth)
    - We are sent forth to be justice workers and peace makers, proclaiming and living out the good news (we carry on the mission of Jesus Christ)
14. We hold a hierarchal value system
    - Some concepts, especially in the field of morality, for example, are more important than others (levels of discernment)
    - Similarly, various parts of the Bible, the catechism, the creeds, and church law have varying degrees of importance and priority

How can this faith perspective help us live our lives better? This is a vision to work toward. Are we there yet—individually or collectively? No! Does this mean that we give up or walk away from this vision? No! We are to engage this vision and integrate it into our lives the best we can. Then slowly we will notice the fruits of this commitment develop into something beautiful and fulfilling for ourselves and for others.

Reflection Questions

1. Has any of the above shocked me or made me feel uncomfortable?
2. What aspects of Catholicism attract me to this perspective of Christianity?
3. What are my priorities as a Catholic?
4. Where do I not live up to these ideals?

Epilogue

And Finally...

The playwright George Bernard Shaw wrote in 1921, "Life wasn't meant to be easy my child, but take courage: it can be delightful." I think most of us would agree that life can be difficult, challenging, sometimes even chaotic. But somewhere in that vast landscape of experiences, relationships, successes, and failures lay gems—moments of delight, memories of goodness, encounters of surprise, if only we open the eyes of our soul to see.

These stories and reflections have just this purpose. They are meant to raise questions, nudge memories, open up vistas. This type of bread serves to enrich the soul as you delve deeper into the interior questions and reflections that come from living your life.

I invite you to look for the delight, the humor, the wisdom hidden in the details of your own life story. There you will find the bread that nourishes your soul, and the lives of all those you encounter. It is my fervent wish that in doing this work, you will discover your way to ever deepening nourishment, healing, and transformation.

Works Cited

Au, Wilkie, and Noreen Cannon Au. *Aging With Wisdom and Grace*. Mahwah, NJ: Paulist Press, 2021.

Au, Wilkie, and Noreen Cannon. *The Discerning Heart: Exploring the Christian Path*. Mahwah, NJ: Paulist Press, 2006.

Blythe, Theresa. *50 Ways to Pray: Practices from Many Traditions and Times*. Nashville: Abingdon Press, 2006.

Boyle, Gregory. *The Whole Heart: The Power of Extravagant Tenderness*. New York: Avid Reader Press, 2021.

Campbell, Joseph. *Pathways to Bliss: Mythology and Personal Transformation*. Novato, CA: New World Library, 2004.

Chapman, Gary. *The 5 Love Languages: The Secret to Love That Lasts*. Chicago: Northfield Park, 1992.

De Mello, Anthony. *Rediscovering Life: Awaken to Reality*. New York: Image, 2012.

Farrell, Edward. *Prayer Is a Hunger*. Denville, NJ: Dimension Books, 1972.

Francis. *Laudato Si'* (2015).

Frankl, Victor. *Man's Search for Meaning*. Boston: Beacon Press, 2006.

Gottman, John. *The Seven Principles for Making Marriage Work*. New York: Harmony Books, 2015.

Hessel, Dieter T. *Maggie Kuhn on Aging: A Dialogue Edited by Dieter Hessel*. Philadelphia: Westminster John Knox Press, 1977.

Hillman, James. *Revisioning Psychology*. New York: Harper Perennial, 1975.

Jaku, Eddie. *The Happiest Man on Earth*. New York: Harper Collins, 2020.

John Paul II. *Laborem Exercens* (1981).

———. *Solicitudo Rei Socialis* (1987).

Lane, Belden. *The Solace of Fierce Landscapes: Exploring Desert and Mountain Landscapes*. New York: Oxford University Press, 1998.

Leo XIII. *Rerum Novarum* (1891).

Love, Patricia, and Steven Stosny. *How to Improve Your Marriage Without Talking About It*. New York: Broadway Books, 2007.

McGirr, Michael. *Things You Get for Free*. Melbourne: Scribe, 2012.

McNuff, Anna. *Fifty Shades of the USA*. Las Vegas, NV, 2018.

Moore, Thomas. *A Life at Work: The Joy of Discovering What You Were Born to Do*. New York: Broadway Books, 2008.

———. *The Re-Enchantment of Everyday Life*. New York: Harper Perennial, 1997.

New American Bible, revised edition, 2011.

Oliver, Mary. *Felicity*. New York: Penguin Press, 2015.

Peterson, Jordan. *12 Rules for Life: An Antidote for Chaos*. New York: Random House, 2018.

Pierce, Gregory. *Spirituality at Work: 10 Ways to Balance Your Life On-the-Job*. Chicago: Loyola Press, 2001.

Ramsey, Dave. *The Total Money Makeover: A Proven Plan for Financial Fitness*. Nashville: Nelson Books, 2013.

Rohr, Richard. *Falling Upward: A Spirituality for the Two Halves of Life*. San Francisco: Jossey-Bass, 2011.

———. *Immortal Diamond: The Search for Our True Self*. San Francisco: Jossey-Bass, 2013.

———. *Why Be Catholic: Understanding Our Experience and Tradition*. Cincinnati: Franciscan Media, 1989.

Shalomi, Zalman Schachter. *From Age-ing to Sage-ing: A Revolutionary Approach to Growing Older.* New York: Warner Books, 1995.

Tannen, Deborah. *You Just Don't Understand: Women and Men in Conversation.* New York: Ballantine Books, 1990.

Teresa of Avila. *The Interior Castle.* Charlotte, NC: St. Benedict Press, 2011.

Thibault, Jane, and Richard Morgan. *Pilgrimage into the Last Third of Life: 7 Gateways to Spiritual Growth.* Nashville: Upper Room Books, 2012.

Thibodeaux, Mark. *God, I Have Issues: 50 Ways to Pray No Matter How You Feel.* Cincinnati: St. Anthony Messenger Press, 2005.

Tolle, Eckhart. *The Power of Now: A Guide to Spiritual Enlightenment.* Novato, CA: New World Library, 1997.

Tornstam, Lars. *Gerotranscendence: A Developmental Theory of Positive Aging.* New York: Springer, 2005.

OTHER BOOKS BY THE AUTHOR

Creating Rituals

A New Way of Healing for Everyday Life

Practical advice on creating rituals, a healing and transformative means of helping a person or a group to maneuver with confidence through times of transition.

978-0-8091-4716-8 $14.95 160 pages

OTHER BOOKS BY THE AUTHOR

Soul-Centered

Spirituality for People on the Go

Specifically aimed at the busy layperson, this book underlines the idea that spirituality is not exotic, something for the few, but that it is in ordinary things and daily life that we can find intimacy with God.

978-0-8091-4919-3 $14.95 144 pages

OTHER BOOKS BY THE AUTHOR

Here Comes Life!

Seeking Wholeness and Happiness

Life happens—with all its questions, longings, challenges, and missteps; but even more importantly, with its constant search for wholeness and happiness. It is not concerned with canonical or theological debates, but with pastoral considerations. *Here Comes Life!* shows the reader how to live out the teachings of Pope Francis in real life.

978-0-8091-5512-5 $14.95 136 pages

OTHER BOOKS BY THE AUTHOR

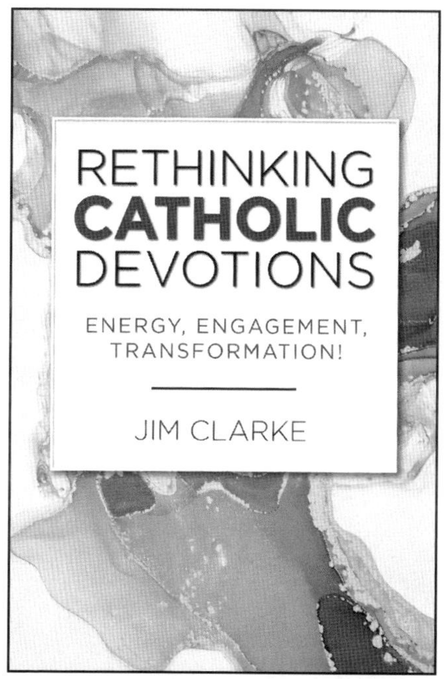

Rethinking Catholic Devotions

Energy, Engagement, Transformation!

A wide-ranging discussion of popular devotionalism as practiced in the U.S. Catholic Church, with a brief history of how devotions arose and ways to rethink them for the 21st century.

978-0-8091-5533-0 $17.95 144 pages